Women Who Don't Wait in Line

Women Who Don't Wait in Line

BREAK THE MOLD, LEAD THE WAY

Reshma Saujani

New Harvest
Houghton Mifflin Harcourt
BOSTON • NEW YORK
2013

This edition published by special arrangement with Amazon Publishing

For information about permission to reproduce selections from this book,
write to Permissions, Houghton Mifflin Harcourt Publishing Company,
215 Park Avenue South, New York, New York 10003.

www.hmhbooks.com

Library of Congress Cataloging-in-Publication Data
Saujani, Reshma.
Women who don't wait in line : break the mold, lead the way / Reshma
Saujani.
pages cm
ISBN 978-0-544-02778-7 (hardback)
1. Women in the professions. 2. Leadership in women. 3. Women
executives. 4. Success in business. I. Title.
HD6054.S38 2013
658.4'09082—dc23   2013027148

Printed in the United States of America
DOC 10 9 8 7 6 5 4 3 2 1

For all the women in my life whose shoulders I stand on,
and for all the women who will stand on mine

It is not the critic who counts; not the [wo]man who points out how the strong [wo]man stumbles, or where the doer of deeds could have done them better. The credit belongs to the [wo]man who is actually in the arena, whose face is marred by dust and sweat and blood; who strives valiantly; who errs, who comes short again and again, because there is no effort without error and shortcomings; but who does actually strive to do the deeds; who knows the great enthusiasms, the great devotions; who spends [herself] in a worthy cause; who at the best knows in the end the triumph of high achievement, and who at the worst, if [s]he fails, at least fails while daring greatly, so that [her] place shall never be with those cold and timid souls who know neither victory nor defeat.

— THEODORE ROOSEVELT (1858–1919), twenty-sixth president of the United States, excerpt from "Citizenship in a Republic," delivered at the Sorbonne, Paris, France, April 23, 1910

CONTENTS

The Most Successful Campaign Ever Lost

I WOKE UP THE day after my congressional election in a hotel room strewn with half-eaten Oreos and three unopened bottles of champagne. The victory party never happened. I had thought I was going to win: The *New York Daily News* endorsed my campaign, the *Wall Street Journal* had snapped pictures of me throughout Election Day, and *CNBC* called my race one of the hottest in the country. I had raised $1.6 million. But in the end, I only got 19 percent of the vote. I had no job, I had pissed off the who's who of the Democratic establishment, and I was broke.

My loss was so public — so humiliating. What would I do now? I had only a victory speech in my purse. No concession speech. No contingency plan.

I wanted to crawl into a ball and stay in the fetal position. Forever.

But I also wanted to get out of the hotel room, which now felt claustrophobic. I gathered the presents, the flowers, and the cards. My field organizers had posted victory notes all over the suite. Yellow, pink, and blue Post-Its — a flourescent garden of good will. Those poor kids: They'd spent ten months of their lives working untiringly for a candidate who got less than a quarter of the vote.

It was not even 8 A.M., and my cell phone was ringing nonstop. The light on my BlackBerry seemed to have turned permanently red, and it was filled with emails I couldn't bear to read. The last thing I wanted to do was speak to anyone. I jumped in a cab and prayed that no one would recognize me.

The day before, I had called everyone I knew and told them that the race was really close — that they had to get all their friends out to vote, because it would be, at best, a five-point spread. Looking at the night's election returns, they must have thought I was the ultimate amateur. And those were my friends. Soon there would be the opinions of non-friends to contend with. Call me psychic, but I suspected the age of virtual *schadenfreude* via Twitter and Google would be unkind to me. For months, publications had referred to me as "the thirty-four-year-old Indian-American upstart" who "audaciously" ran against the "eighteen-year incumbent." I could only imagine the gleeful Google alerts: *"Saujani spends $1.6 million and just gets 19 percent of the vote. Tom Delay got more votes on Dancing with the Stars."*

After what seemed like an eternity, I made it back to my apartment on the Lower East Side. Still wearing the same crumpled suit I had on the night before, I crawled into bed for my second big cry of the day. For the first time ever, I was thankful that my six-by-nine bedroom lacked windows. Darkness had never looked so good.

But despite the comfort of home and my extreme exhaustion, I couldn't sleep. I had let so many people down: my field organizers, my donors and supporters, my family, my friends, peers, and the people who I had met on the campaign trail who thought I would be the breakthrough candidate. The residents at the public housing development whose support I won would be so disappointed. I had spent my life savings in the process. Big questions were flashing through my head. *How had I lost? What would I do now?*

You can only sleep and hide and cry for so long. The next morning, I willed myself from under the covers to the sound of rushing traffic. I collected the path of crumpled tissues filling my room, and began to face my defeat.

I was sure of a few things: I was grateful to my supporters; and, even after a humiliating loss, I was still dedicated to pursuing public service. That was my story — my truth — and I was ready to present it to the world. Or, at least I was ready to face the blinking red light on my phone.

I went through my BlackBerry and listened to my voicemails. The first one was left at 8 A.M. by a community activist. "I am so proud of you. The future has many, many great things ahead of you, and I know that you will have nothing but great success moving forward," she said.

Her message gave me the strength to start returning calls. I began what I thought would be a painful, embarrassing process of apologizing to my supporters for letting them down. But I was shocked to find out that they weren't upset or disappointed in me. *They were proud of me.*

A surprising number of people offered some unexpected perspective: "Your loss will make you stronger . . . ," "You have a bright future and the key now is to pick yourself up, dust yourself off, and approach failure with enthusiasm," "You had the courage to run for the next generation and you were running on ideas, not incumbency, and you should be proud of that."

People actually congratulated me. I was stunned, moved, and heartened. They said their support was an investment: a down payment on what I could contribute to our community and country in the next ten years. After speaking with my supporters, reading emails, and collecting advice, I realized my career in public service wasn't over. It was just beginning.

Some people have known since they were kids that they wanted to become doctors and lawyers and astronauts. As long as I can remember, I've wanted to be a public servant. Sure, it may have seemed to some observers as if I got up one morning, drank a cup of grapefruit juice, and declared on a whim — "Hey, I think I'll run for Congress today." But in truth it was a desire that's been a part of my entire life. I've always been a political junkie and an activist. Public service is my calling, and I'm grateful for that.

My first introduction to activism — and the thrilling power of building a movement to effect change — was when I was 13. I grew up in Schaumburg, Illinois, a medium-sized town in the Midwest, which, in the 1980s, had few minority families. My parents had come to Illinois after being expelled from Uganda by the dictator Idi Amin. It was hardly an epicenter of cultural diversity, and racism was rampant. I was no stranger to being harassed about my ethnicity. One day after school I got beaten up with a baseball bat after some kids called me a *haji*. I can't count the number of times I was asked whether my mother was born with a dot on her head. These experiences motivated me to do something to fight back. But I was still a young girl and barely four-foot-seven — hardly an intimidating presence.

I had to retaliate in a different way and use other tactics to incite change. I asked a teacher if I could start a student organization. I called it PRISM (Prejudice Reduction Interested Students Movement), and started on a mission to teach my classmates about other cultures. It attracted fifty other students, and we sponsored a cultural show at the end of the year. It made me realize that with a group of supporters, together we could create change with a lasting impact. (The group, now called the Diversity Club, still exists at my high school.)

College only heightened my interest in activism. During my first week as a freshman at the University of Illinois, I watched a group of students galvanize in response to a slew of racial slurs that had been graffitied on campus. They gave speeches on the quad. They marched and chanted slogans. I was in awe of their ability to mobilize hundreds of people for their cause. I was particularly energized by the fearlessness of a young woman who stood in front of the crowd and gave a passionate speech. I wanted to do that: I wanted to be able to move people to action and bring people together to create change.

I immersed myself in politics and spent my college years organizing students against the Republicans' Contract with America, then–Speaker of the House Newt Gingrich's platform of extreme conservative politics. I worked to demand diversity centers on campus. I helped organize a group of Asian Americans who fought for an Asian American Studies program and a Cultural House at the University of Illinois. (Both were created by the time I graduated and both remain on campus today.)

But I longed to work on a real political campaign, and in 1996 I got my chance. I arrived in Washington, D.C., just shy of twenty-one, and was mesmerized by the political consciousness that infused the capital city. I felt at home. I interned in the White House during the day, working at the Office of Public Engagement, and spent my evenings working on Asian American outreach for the Clinton-Gore re-election campaign. I had enjoyed being involved in Asian American issues in college and it was fulfilling to work on these issues on a national stage.

At my first political event in D.C., I was entranced by everyone's buttons: "Asian Americans for Clinton-Gore;" "Women for Clinton-Gore;" "LBGT for Clinton-Gore." It seemed as though people from disparate backgrounds were coming together for the first time to have a discussion about the state of our nation. And I desperately wanted to be a part of that conversation. Moreover, I wanted to help drive it forward.

The best way to start down that path, I thought at the time, was to go to Yale Law School after I graduated from college. I applied; I was rejected. And, of course, I was devastated. Considering my options, I decided to set my sights on the Kennedy School of Government at Harvard instead. Leafing through the course guide I saw the perfect class: "How to Win Your First Election." I thought to myself, "Sign me up!!!"

I entered the Kennedy School of Government in the fall of 1997 as the youngest student in the class. After the first week, it was painfully obvious that I was completely lost. Instead of going to classes on grass-roots organizing, I was learning about statistical regression analysis. One day, after a particularly frustrating class, I found myself wondering if my parents had been right to question my decision to go to the Kennedy School.

Compounding these worries were financial concerns. My disapproving parents had cut me off financially. I was sleeping on a friend's couch on Beacon Street in Boston and I needed a job to help pay for rent, as my Perkins loans were certainly not putting food on the table. Looking for solutions, I picked up a newsletter and discovered a job opening for a research assistant for Judge A. Leon Higginbotham Jr.: one of the most prominent civil rights jurists in the country. I applied.

When I met Judge Higginbotham during my interview, he told me the story of *his* first job interview. The Judge, as we referred to him, attended Yale Law School and after graduation in

1952 he scored interviews from all of the top law firms. When he showed up at the first one, however, the recruiting partner realized that he was black and told him that they had no place for him. The Judge told me when he walked out of the prestigious firm — a firm at which he had aspired to work, a place where he deserved a spot — he sat down on the steps and cried. All that he could think about was his mother who cleaned houses to put him through law school. I was in awe of the Judge's candor and perseverance, and I knew that he was going to be my mentor and guide through the next two years of my life.

Judge Higginbotham taught his staff not to be "part of the problem," but to be "part of the rational solution to eradicate racial discrimination in America." Every Sunday he would gather his interns and research assistants and invite legal crusaders to speak to us, including Charles Ogletree, the founder of Harvard Law School's Charles Hamilton Houston Institute for Race and Justice, and D.C. Delegate Eleanor Holmes Norton. They would share their stories, and we would soak it all up.

I confided in the Judge my burning desire to attend Yale Law School and that I had been rejected. He encouraged me not to give up. He taught me to dream big and not to wait in line.

I was ten years old when I first decided I wanted to go to Yale Law School. After watching the movie *The Accused,* in which Kelly McGillis plays a district attorney representing a rape victim, I decided I wanted to become a lawyer. I asked my father to take me to the library and I looked up the rankings of top law schools in *U.S. News and World Report.* Even in 1987, the top school was Yale Law School. I asked my dad to photocopy the list. I highlighted Yale Law School with my yellow Hello Kitty marker and taped it on our refrigerator when we got home. I would stare at the little paper daily—a constant reminder of what I wanted to achieve.

I applied to Yale Law School two more times between 1996 and 2000. With each rejection my father lamented the day he let me tape up that piece of paper on the refrigerator. When I received my third rejection letter I took a train to New Haven from Cambridge, where I was still at the Kennedy School, and knocked on Dean Kronman's door. Clutching that tattered 1987 article from *U.S. News and World Report* that I had attached to my fridge so many years ago, I made a passionate pitch as to why he should let me into Yale. I told him that I wasn't taking no for an answer. He stared at me, seeing the determination in my eyes. He told me to attend any of the other schools that had accepted me. If I got into the top 10 percent of my class, then he would let me transfer. I reluctantly agreed. With hard work and determination, I completed my first year of law school at Georgetown and entered Yale the following fall. I refused to let failure stop me from achieving my dream to go to Yale Law School.

Yale was all I hoped it would be and more. But when I graduated, I was over $200,000 in student loan debt. So instead of immediately pursuing my dream of public service, I accepted a job at Davis Polk and Wardwell, a white-shoe law firm in New York City, so I could pay off my student loan debt and help my parents with their finances.

I owe my decision to run for Congress to one group of amazing women. I was sitting in the house of one of Hillary Clinton's biggest supporters and a leader in the women's movement in New York, during a meeting of the Eleanor Roosevelt Legacy Committee. I mentioned that I was leaving my job at Fortress

Investment Group for Washington, D.C., shortly to interview at the State Department. All of the women gave me a funny look and said, "Why are you going to D.C. to interview for the State Department? You should run for office in New York."

At the time, veteran Congresswoman Carolyn Maloney had been contemplating a run against Kirsten Gillibrand, the junior senator who had been selected by President Obama to fill Hillary's Senate seat when she transitioned to the State Department. If Maloney ran for Senate, her congressional seat would be open. In a town where people live and die in their seats, this was a huge opportunity. Still, I shook my head at what seemed to be impossible — there was no way that I could run. Although I wanted to dedicate my life to public service and had wanted to run for elected office since I moved to New York, it seemed as though year after year I would find another reason to put it off. New York politics always felt so scary. Too hard. Too dirty. Too competitive. Moreover, I didn't have the three traditional elements of electability: (1) I was not a current elected official seeking higher office; (2) I had no money, I had debt; and (3) I had no name recognition (not to mention a funnier-sounding name than Barack Obama).

I appreciated their vote of confidence. But I still assumed that I had to pursue my dream in a more established way, a "proper way."

But I had dedicated years to electing progressive leaders, and had formulated an array of policy ideas on job creation, education, innovation, energy efficiency, and foreign policy. I was frustrated that my generation was inheriting an economic mess and yet we didn't have a seat at the table to find solutions.

I thought that if I was elected I could get stuff done, but I kept making excuses for why I couldn't or shouldn't. I was succumbing to my fear that it was just simply too hard.

But wasn't everything worth doing too hard? Could it be harder than graduating Harvard? Or harder than getting into Yale? I had failed at that three times, but I never considered not trying. Maybe the "proper way," the established way — waiting in line, paying my dues — maybe *that* way was passé.

For years I had been attending events at the Women's Campaign Forum and Emily's List, an organization that helps get women elected. The leadership consistently urged young women and women of color to run for Congress. Didn't I fit the bill? I had attended countless panels where women in elected office would look into the audience and tell us to run. Did they mean it? And even if they didn't mean it, didn't it mean something to me?

When the State Department offered me a job in D.C., I had a difficult choice to make: Accept an amazing post or run for a congressional seat that wasn't fully open yet. Carolyn Maloney had not made a final decision, and if she decided to bag the Senate campaign and stick with defending her seat in Congress, I would be running against an eighteen-year incumbent in a Democratic primary.

I called my dad, terrified he would tell me not to run because it would financially burden the family. He surprised me. I revealed my dream to quit my job and run for office and he simply replied, "Finally."

On November 5, 2009, my exploratory campaign became official. I emailed my friends and professional contacts, announcing my run for Congress.

Many people were excited and energized about what I was setting out to do. But to my surprise, the response from some women in the Democratic establishment was mixed — hostile, even.

I had thought I would be applauded for having the audacity to run. I had thought I would be praised for doing what the established Democratic women's groups were always urging young women — particularly young women of color — to do. But my "upstart" status was viewed as an abomination — the reflection of an ambitious young woman who didn't know her place. I was literally told it wasn't my "turn." I was told that I had to "wait in line."

Powerful women said it was a mistake to run against another woman. That I should run against a man instead — and preferably, one they didn't like.

A prominent former elected official, for whom I'd always had the greatest admiration and respect, called my finance chair to tell her to tell me to get out of the race. She said that it was not my turn and ordered me to get in the back of the line. How could it be, I wondered, that she could have this view of our democratic system? How could she prefer a system of coronation where established leaders would crown their successors?

I even received intimidating emails from former leaders of prominent women's organizations. I didn't understand — and still don't understand — why those working for women's equality were so opposed to my run. Haven't we arrived at a point where women should be encouraged to pursue political office? Where women in fact have so many opportunities that they can run against one another — not run a campaign in which gender is the biggest issue? Why wasn't there room for both of us to run, and an understanding that the best woman should win?

Ultimately, I did not let my detractors dissuade me from running. I got thousands of people to sign up to my website and raised $400,000 in less than two months, with early fundraising help from the Grammy-winning musician John Legend and Twitter cofounder Jack Dorsey. The campaign made it to the front page of the *New York Times* and the *Washington Post*. We were named one of the top ten races in the country by CNBC. I got key endorsements — from the *New York Observer* and the *Daily News*, the largest paper in New York. Perhaps my most emotional moment during the campaign was when an eighty-year-old Indian man approached me in the subway and told me he had lived in the U.S. for half his life and never voted before, but he was registering so that he could vote for me. I was humbled and deeply moved.

I gave the campaign everything I had, and in the end, I lost. It was the worst thing I could have anticipated. And yet, it was the best thing that has ever happened to me.

I lost the election, but I gained insight into what is holding women back — and what we need to do to propel them ahead. This book is the story not only of my experience, but also the experiences of countless women of my generation. We all have an inner activist. Consider this a call to action, an anthem to inspire women and enlist them in remaking America. But in order to do so we must change how we think about leadership, how we apply for jobs, how we teach our daughters, what we dream, and how we go for it. We must teach ourselves not to wait, that our time is now.

Any woman who dares to dream big has likely been told that to succeed she has to be better, smarter, and more prepared than her male counterpart. But the "better, smarter, and more prepared" mantra comes with a cost. It dissuades women from taking risks — and that's dangerous.

As we continue to move toward an innovation economy,

success will be rewarded not by pedigree, but by personal experience, including both triumphs and failures. Women now make up more than half of all college students, but we are seeing gender-equity stagnation at the top levels of leadership.[1] The new leaders of companies are not Harvard grads, but college dropouts who had an idea and pursued it in their own ways. Women will be better prepared and better positioned if we are encouraged to follow our own path instead of a predetermined one. After all, it's not by adhering to an existing route that we discover a better way — it's by deviating from it.

The time has come to disrupt and rebuild the existing model of leadership. We must challenge previous notions of what the path to success should look like.

We're quick to blame the problem on men: The rules have been established by men to their own advantage, or innate male traits, like egoism or being aggressive, allow men to get ahead because they are traits women lack. However, neither of these reasons is the sole cause of our modern-day conundrum. It's not only men who are holding us back: It's ourselves.

Young women in particular are being asked to operate with a twentieth-century mentality in a twenty-first-century economy. The old, last-century paradigm urges us to go slower, to be careful and cautious, to wait our turn. But that paradigm is broken. We need to change it, or women will never achieve full parity and equality in American society.

In the following pages, I provide a new model for the next generation of leadership. The seven chapters explore lessons I learned and include stories from incredible women who are closing the gender gap, who didn't get bogged down by wanting to be liked, and who found the right support network and the right teams to help them fulfill their dreams. *Women Who Don't Wait in Line* is a wakeup call for us to start thinking differently about the next generation of leadership. It illuminates how the old model of feminism is holding us back, and it advocates a new model that encourages competition, promotes taking risks over fear of failure, building support networks and sisterhoods, and frees us from feeling like we have to dress like men. Because after all, we are not men, and it is time to stop pretending we want to be. We must find strength in our gender instead of trying to hide or apologize for it. We don't have to emanate the over-prepared, know-it all caricature of the "ambitious woman." We should be comfortable embracing authentic, softer styles of leadership, because there is no one-size-fits-all model. We can be anything, and being a woman has very little to do with it. Each chapter incorporates the counsel of women who don't wait in line — women who run the world or who are poised to do so. It illuminates a new path, one with bends and curves but room for everyone to achieve her destiny and change the world. This book offers a path that is governed by sponsorship, that has women walking down it together, holding each other up, lending a hand — or a gentle push — to help one another get ahead.

I am writing this book because we need you to get engaged to make our world better. If that's your dream, I'm here to tell you: Jump the line. The time for waiting is over.

Women Who Don't Wait in Line

1

Fail Fast, Fail First, Fail Hard

IN JANUARY 2010, when I officially announced my decision to run for Congress, so many years after first having dreamed the idea, I expected to feel an overwhelming sense of relief and excitement.

Instead, to my surprise, I was racked with anxiety. Heart-pounding, ear-buzzing, stomach-churning anxiety. Often, as I was heading to important meetings, I'd find myself in a cold sweat.

Why, now that I was doing what I'd always wanted, was I feeling so panicked? It wasn't that I questioned my own commitment — I wanted this job to make a difference more than anything. But nagging voices of self-doubt were echoing in my hand. Critics were charging that I was too young, too new, too different, too inexperienced. I got bogged down in how others saw me, and started losing sight of myself. What if I flubbed a policy question? Would I be dismissed as a lightweight? Did I have the chops, the smarts, the skills to handle this job?

In retrospect, my insecurities seem unwarranted. Sure, I was younger than my opponent — but, at thirty-four, hardly a fledgling. After all, there are numerous examples of even younger men who have been elected to the House of Representatives.

For example, Aaron Schock, who at twenty-seven ran and won an election to represent Illinois's Eighteenth Congressional District in 2009.

As for being a lightweight, I had a master's degree in public policy from Harvard and a law degree from Yale. And I wasn't a newbie to the political world: I had a decade of campaign experience working on presidential and local elections, and I had seen scores of candidates go through the firing squad of dense policy questions, so I knew what to expect. I'd been a civic activist, organizing young people and communities of color since I was thirteen years old. But in the moment, instead of focusing on all the things I knew that I knew, I stressed about what I didn't know. Instead of feeling confident in who I was, I fretted about who — and what — I was not.

To manage my anxiety, I obsessed over my stump speech. The speech became a symbol of something I could control and perfect and use to mitigate my chances of losing the race. I convinced myself that if I could memorize the lines, and gracefully deliver each word, then somehow that polished performance would smooth over any perceived flaws. I spent hours in front of the computer, watching speech after speech on YouTube, trying to discern the secrets of great orators like Eleanor Roosevelt or Benazir Bhutto. I imagined delivering the speech in my head, over and over again. The perfect speech was going to become a stand-in for a perfect me.

On the day of a speech, I would pace up and down the length of my apartment, clutching the script, rehearsing my arguments before the empty room. Then, at game time, I would take a crumpled sheet of speech notes with me, keeping them at the podium, in a pocket, or in my purse, like Linus's security blanket — a safeguard against the prospect that I might forget an important line.

My communications director kept scolding me for obsessing about memorization. "It isn't how you say it," he'd argue. "It's what you have to say." It took time for his words to sink in, but I finally came around.

By the end of the campaign trail, I had tossed the cheat sheet. No more trying to adhere to a faultless script. I spoke from the heart — about who I was, what I believed, and what I would do for my community if elected. I stopped trying to be perfect and just started to be me: all of me, even the part of me that occasionally fumbles words, trips over my tongue, or sometimes sounds inelegant. And I ultimately learned that having confidence in myself — believing that I was prepared enough, smart enough, and strong enough — was not only empowering, but it was also a self-fulfilling prophecy. I became these things. And confidence is also infectious, because that's when my campaign took off. That's when other people became passionately drawn to our call for change.

Take the Leap

Women tend to underestimate their own abilities, while men tend to overestimate theirs. This phenomenon even affects women who have managed to overcome their insecurities, taken professional risks, and are at the height of their careers.

Women are taught to be risk-averse. Starting at a young age, we are taught to stay off the monkey bars, stay in the shallow end — with the result that too often, we prepare and prepare instead of boldly pursuing our dreams. Women take classes on everything from how to start a business to making investments, while men just forge ahead. Maybe that's part of the reason why women seem stalled in the corporate hierarchy; why, even as there has been an explosion of women in management positions, so few are making it all the way to the top. And why, when women get to the top, they stay there, instead of taking even more risks to get to the next leadership level.

Take, for example, Virginia M. Rometty, who became CEO of IBM in January 2012. Rometty is outspoken about the importance of her willingness to take both personal and professional risks. She attributes her career success to "experiential" learning and her willingness to try to learn from new things. Nonetheless, the *New York Times* reported that when Rometty was offered the "big job," she felt she lacked experience and would need time to consider the position.[1]

When she discussed the offer with her husband, he asked her, "Do you think a man would have ever answered that question that way?"

Rometty realized that not only was she qualified and ready for the job, but it was exactly the kind of challenge she needed to push herself even further. "People are their first worst critic, and it stops them from getting another experience," she observed. It's a vicious cycle: Women give themselves more time to improve their skills, to gain one more qualification, and, as a result, they may pass up that promotion and the challenges that come with it, which is exactly what they need to grow professionally. According to Rometty, "Growth and comfort do not coexist."[2]

Never hide. Learn by doing. I did not become a better speaker, and ultimately a better candidate, by waiting to ripen like fruit in a brown paper bag. I evolved by stepping out into the world and responding to the cues and feedback around me. I learned how to run for office by running for office. I learned how to be a compelling public speaker by speaking publicly. I evolved by taking big risks in pursuit of a big goal, knowing fully that I might fail.

Anxiety about whether we're ready for the big challenge is a recurring theme and often leads women down the road of endless preparation, the pursuit of perfection, and the desire to prove we can do the job before we even dare to apply. My obsession with memorizing my stump speech fell into this category. I didn't want to screw up or flub my first impression with voters. I was afraid that if I stumbled in my speech, the audience would conclude I wasn't smart — and that, by the same token, a perfect delivery would be equated in their minds with a perfect candidate. So I practiced and practiced, rehearsed and rehearsed, and almost drove myself nuts in the process.

I'm not saying that women should be content with a subpar performance. But too often, the effect of holding ourselves to such high standards is that we forgo the chance to show our mettle at all. Either we hang back because we're afraid we won't excel, or we content ourselves with baby steps in our careers, instead of taking ambitious leaps.

This leads to the second issue that modern women must confront: getting comfortable with risk-taking.

There is a time to take risks and a time to hedge your bets. For example, during the financial crisis, it was striking that there were no top female decision makers at any major Wall Street firm. It made me wonder, as many others did too: If Lehman Brothers had been Lehman Sisters, would the company still be around today? If more women ran Wall Street, would the financial crisis have happened or been as catastrophic?

Evidence shows that this aversion to risk actually leads to higher investment returns when women are the ones making investment decisions. Professors Brad Barber and Terrance Odean found that women's portfolios outperform men's portfolios by about 1 percent annually.[3] Female investors trade in and out of stocks less frequently and avoid investment decisions that are more volatile.

That's courage—and we need more of it. When our cautious instincts become intertwined with excessive doubt about our own abilities and qualifications, we are thwarting our potential and holding ourselves back from reaching new levels of success. It's hard to win the race when women opt out before we even get to the starting line.

A few years ago I read a story about the GNOME Project, which designs free and open-source software. The company advertised for a summer coding position and received almost two hundred applications—all of them from men. An observer might conclude that there simply weren't any capable female programmers for the job. But the article went on to explain, "When GNOME advertised an identical program for women, emphasizing opportunities for learning and mentorship instead of tough competition, it received applications from more than 100 highly qualified females."[4]

Anna Lewis, who wrote the article and also recruited talent for a private-sector software company, recounted her surprise at learning from a female intern that the corporation's slogan—"We Help the World's Best Developers Make Better Software"—might alienate female candidates, because, as the intern put it, "when you hear the phrase 'the world's best developers,' you see a guy."[5] How many times does this scenario play out—where capable women withdraw themselves from consideration for a position before they even apply?

There is an elephant in the room that we all need to get over: the fear of failure. No one likes failing—but women may take the prospect especially hard. Tiffany Dufu, an inspirational leader who ran the White House Project and is now the chief leadership officer of Levo League, credits her father with helping her overcome fear of failure from a very early age:

> I got lots of practice very early doing a couple of things that are very challenging for women to do in terms of their leadership trajectory. One is I had to fail all the time publicly in front of people because if I wasn't always going to win my student government election, I still had to come to school the next day having lost the race or lost the election.[6]

Of course, it's too late for us to turn back the clock and run for elementary school student government, but there is much we can do to help one another assert the confidence to lead — and raise our daughters to trust their own voices, as Tiffany's dad did.

After all, the world's most successful women have not achieved what they have achieved by avoiding failure. Many did not succeed the first, second, or even third time they tried for a big goal. But they kept at it, they kept pushing. Gertrude Stein submitted poem after poem for twenty years before one was accepted by a publication. Oprah Winfrey had a rocky start to her professional career and was fired for "being 'unfit for TV.'"[7] Marilyn Monroe was dropped from Twentieth Century–Fox one year into her contract and was told that she was not pretty and had no future in acting. Emily Dickinson had only a dozen of the more than eighteen hundred poems she wrote published during her lifetime. J. K. Rowling, the author of the best-selling Harry Potter book series, was a single mother living on welfare before her book was sold. Kathryn Stockett received sixty rejection letters for her novel *The Help*. Lady Gaga got dropped by a label early in her career. The list goes on.

- Ladies, it's time to stop worrying and start believing.
- Everything you know and are is enough to snag that promotion; you are more capable than you give yourself credit for.
- Never hide. Learn by doing.
- Nothing wagered, nothing gained — it pays to take risks.
- Get comfortable with failure. It's a necessary part of progress.

JUMP THE LINE

Throw a Failure Party

One of the best ways to bolster your confidence is to realize you're not alone. The prospect of failure seems less scary when you know that women you admire have stumbled — or worse — and not just survived but thrived. So throw a Failure Party. Invite friends, colleagues, neighbors, people you admire to share the stories of their own mistakes. Ask all of your guests to prepare a two-minute story about their biggest failure to share with the room. Let's get over our aversion to admitting or reflecting on failure. Truth-telling in this way is empowering.

It's also refreshing. I mean, how many times have you heard panelists or presenters go on and on about all the things they got right without mentioning one thing about what they did wrong? It's boring and unhelpful. Worse, half the time, those panels just make you feel bad about yourself.

The universal truth is that achieving success isn't something that happens on a first try. It's hard work for everyone. Women and men are failing around us all the time. As aspiring leaders, what we really want to know is how they ran their car off the track — and what they did to get back in the race.

To build an army of strong women we must be willing to admit our struggles to one another. Stephanie Harbour, the former president of Mom Corps NYC, sees failure as an opportunity to connect and support other women.

> I really try to encourage young women that failure is okay — especially if you are the kind of woman who strives for excellence and almost always succeeds. You get into good schools. You do well at those schools. You get good jobs. And then you have a big failure and it can be absolutely devastating. Women fail silently a lot and suffer silently. [Instead,] we can help each other learn and be more open about those failures; that's a huge area of opportunity for us to help pick each other up in pretty big ways.

Here's the plan: Get a bunch of friends, colleagues, and mentors together for a meal and have a conversation about mistakes you've made and what you could have or should have done differently. Be vulnerable. Be honest. Let it all hang out. There is no shame in bearing your battle scars.

Angel investor and start-up adviser Joanne Wilson told a revealing story at the 2012 ITP's Women Entrepreneurs Festival about how one of the women on the panel was asked a question about the first year of her business. Joanne said, "You hear from most entrepreneurs that everything is just great. There is this eternal optimism. The panelist said she pretty much cried every day of the first year. There was an audible sigh in the room."[8]

I know the idea of celebrating failure may seem kind of weird. Talking about failure is emotionally unpleasant; reliving low moments — yours or anyone else's — may not sound like how you want to spend a Saturday night. But some of the most innovative people in the world — scientists, entrepreneurs, inventors, designers — depend on this very approach. When they are looking at a product, they focus on the flaws. They know that sometimes, the biggest leaps forward begin with understanding what is wrong. We can learn a lot from being more scientific about our failures. We can stop fearing that big fat F word and start seeing failure as badge of courage and a springboard for professional growth.

In fact, several supporters declared that my loss in the New York congressional race was a blessing in disguise. I needed to experience failure in order to ultimately achieve my goals. I know now they were right.

Visualize — and Leap

You know you are on the right path when you are scared as hell.

Going for gold means you may never eradicate all of your fears, and that's okay. Part of life is learning how to force yourself forward even though you are terrified. The truth is, once you get out there, your fear will recede. What we imagine is often much worse than the reality. So don't let your doubts get in the way: Take a deep breath and take that first step.

When you visualize yourself doing something, you're halfway there to making it happen. By the same token, anticipating possible outcomes helps you prepare for whatever lies ahead. I don't know about you, but I don't like surprises. I want to see what's coming. We can't know the future — but by visualizing what *could* happen, we can summon the strength we need to move ahead, even in the face of uncertainty.

When I was considering running for Congress, I knew what the critics might say: that I was inexperienced, ambitious, an upstart, an opportunist. That I didn't stand a chance. But I forced myself to visualize the worst-case scenario. What would failure really mean? I could lose the race. I could be ostracized by party insiders. I could jeopardize my political future. I could go broke. I could lose my idealism. My hair could turn prematurely white.

I ran through every nightmarish scenario and asked myself if I could handle it. The answer was always yes. I realized I could do it, so I decided to run. I knew I'd always regret it if I didn't.

I didn't suddenly become fearless. I simply realized that I was *brave enough* to handle even the worst of outcomes.

And guess what? A lot of the worst-case scenarios did happen, and I'm still standing. Not only that, I'm standing tall. (Okay, I'm five foot six, in heels.) Yes, I lost my first race. But I've gained a great deal by taking a risk, and have even been rewarded by others. I was included in a list of the top Women to Watch in Politics; as the article noted, I landed myself "on the front page of . . . [the] *Washington Post*, quite a feat for the daughter of Indian immigrants who didn't, in her words, wait in line."[9] But the greatest reward has been hearing from women around the country who are now considering running for office for the first time too.

When you are presented with a risky situation like a new job offer, ask yourself: What is the worst that can happen? What do you really have to lose? Often, once you start thinking through your fears, you discover they're not so scary after all. Or, at least, that you are brave enough to deal with whatever life might throw your way.

Do the Thing You Think You Cannot Do

In the great book *The War of Art*, author Steven Pressfield writes, "The more scared we are of a work or calling, the more sure we can be that we have to do it."[10] We can't let fear obstruct our engagement in the things we care about most. Overcoming those fears can be extraordinarily empowering and allow us to take a stand, to speak up, and to be heard.

This point was driven home for me after I lost my election. I was broke and humiliated and trying to figure out what to do with my life. I knew that I didn't want to go back to the private sector, as tempting as that was given my financial situation. Regardless of the outcome, I had loved every moment of running for office. That experience demonstrated to me that public service was what I wanted to spend my life doing.

But how would that knowledge help me pick up the pieces after my fall? I was terrified to go back out there and ask the very elected officials who had endorsed my opponent to give me a job. I thought they would slam the door in my face. But I made myself do it. The race had put me on a new path — the right path — and I wanted to continue. It wasn't about me anymore; it was about my commitment to others. That gave me courage. Putting myself out there again led to an opportunity to serve as the deputy public advocate of New York City. Had I not overcome my fear of rejection, I would never have been able to land a role that I found meaningful and one that allowed me to help immigrant entrepreneurs access capital, or undocumented students obtain scholarships.

I draw inspiration from Susan Lyne, the former president of Gilt Groupe, the e-commerce site that pioneered flash sales. Susan's career has been characterized by taking big risks. "I always applied for jobs I was not qualified for," says Susan. She began her career as an assistant at *City* magazine, an understaffed organization, where she made the case to be promoted to associate editor, even though she had absolutely no training or experience. "As an assistant I had sat in all of the story meetings and

I learned by watching. I also learned that if you don't ask, you don't get. So I asked and I got."

Susan's confidence in her own abilities propelled her to take the risk of applying for an influential job, and by doing so she succeeded in advancing her career. This single experience informed many of the professional decisions she would make throughout her career, and all because she wasn't afraid to take a leap of faith in herself.

Apply for the Job You Think You Are Not Qualified For

If you haven't failed before in your life, it means you haven't taken enough risks. Period. And if you haven't taken enough risks, you're not living up to your true potential. If you cannot think of a professional failure, here is what I want you to do: Imagine your dream job. Write it down, and tomorrow go out and apply for that job. If you are not happy in your industry or your dream job does not exist, write a business plan.

Not enough women are taking these leaps. According to a 2012 Accenture survey, 47 percent of Gen Y women feel they are not progressing and that lack of opportunities and a clear career path are holding them back.[11] I say it's time to start blazing our own paths. It's time to start creating our own opportunities.

Luckily, there are women who can show us how to be bolder, and more creative, in how we manage our own careers.

Another great role model is Libby Brittain, a former associate for the investment firm Hearst Ventures (she's now director of editorial development at the start-up Branch). Libby shared the strategy she used to get her exciting position there: "Hearst Ventures wanted someone with four to five years of business experience in financial consulting. I didn't have either of those, but I did have three years spent at two technology start-ups and two at the *New York Times*. Hearst Ventures is a digital media venture capital investment firm. So I figured out a story that everyone else didn't have."

Sometimes a fresh approach can lead to better results for an organization. Coming into a job without preconceived notions enables you to innovate and excel. Vivien Labaton, the founding director of the Third Wave Foundation, which is a philanthropic fund that supports programs for young feminist activists between the ages of fifteen and thirty, recalls:

> When I got involved with Third Wave, it was going from an idea to an organization, and I remember thinking (and I was twenty-one at the time and the founders were, I don't know, in their mid- to late twenties), "I don't know why we think we can just, like, start an organization like that. That's something that older people do." People at other organizations would say to me, "Wow, you guys have accomplished so much and you've done so much." My response was always, "Well, honestly half the young women that work for you who are administrative assistants could do the same thing if you just gave them the opportunity."

This is not to say that you should have a drastically unrealistic sense of your qualifications and capabilities. Maybe you're not ready to email your boss and tell him you want his job. (Fair enough.) But get to the place where you will be ready to apply for that dream job — and don't be shy about taking the bold steps that will get you ready.

Richelle Parham, the chief marketing officer of eBay, says, "You have to have a sense of where you want to go, even if you don't know exactly what job title you are coveting." Before eBay,

Richelle worked at the advertising agency Digitas, and she knew she wanted to become a general manager. Although she knew she had the requisite skills, she also understood the job was many rungs above her position in the company hierarchy. But she applied for it anyway. She didn't get it, but she got something else: recognition, and a hand. Her then boss approached her and said, "Let me teach you the steppingstones you need to prepare you for the general manager job." It wasn't long before she was promoted.

As you aim to advance in your career, stop taking those professional baby steps and lay down some bold steppingstones instead. Take stretch assignments that will prepare you for the job you want. Try a "double career jump": Figure out the next logical step in your career and apply for the position above it. A goal will always feel out of reach until you challenge yourself to reach for it. In the meantime, get the support you need. Tell your bosses about your professional aspirations, because, as the Gilt Groupe's Susan Lyne's story shows, you can't get it unless you ask for it. Most important, accept the reality that along the way up, you will inevitably take some falls.

Some might argue that punching above our weight is a symptom of an impatient generation, a generation that wants instant gratification and expects things to happen too quickly. It's true that nothing beats hard work, and I'm the first to agree that we have to be willing to put in the time and effort to learn our craft.

But there's another side to this story: There is real value in being eager to contribute even when you are not an expert. Raphaela Sapire is cofounder of the documentary video project Route by Route, which asks women across the country what it means to be a woman in the twenty-first century. She explains:

I think that in some way, if it's even small, I have something to offer and to give, so I just jump in even when I don't have the expertise or all the boxes checked. Probably a lot of what's driving the impatience that [older generations] might perceive is that we have been taught to just say that we have something to offer and to feel genuinely that we have something to give.

Let's go for those big jobs. If we don't get them the first time, we'll know what we need to do next time to succeed.

Fake It till You Make It

Women who don't wait in line live by this mantra. The reality is that many of the opportunities you will get in your professional life are new and have probably never been done before. So fake it, fake it, fake it. Figure it out as you go along. If you are committed and persistent, you still may fail along the way, but you will pick yourself up and learn from it. Men do this all the time. They take on responsibilities they may not be able to handle, but they go for it without worrying about the consequences.

Stephanie Harbour agrees. She believes that:

Women have a tendency to overthink and we're multitaskers by nature. We are very rational. We are very practical and we want to set ourselves up for success. What I found, when I was in banking, was when I was given the option to work on a new project, I oftentimes would kind of weigh what I currently had going on, what I thought I could take on, how realistic I thought the time commitment was, and then would give my realistic answer. I was the only person doing that. Every other person, because they were all men, was coming in and saying, "Yes, I want to work on it." And they were figuring out how they would do it later.

Toughen Up

In 2006, Nina Jacobson, a prominent producer at Disney, was fired over the phone by her male boss while she was still in the delivery room awaiting the birth of her third child. Jacobson responded in an interview with *Newsweek*: "If you're a bullfighter, you expect to get gored periodically. You just hope that you can get up and do it again. I don't feel sorry for myself."[12] She went on to launch her own production company and to bring the best-selling novels *Diary of a Wimpy Kid* and *The Hunger Games* to the screen.

Gilt's Susan Lyne believes that the key indicator for success in life is your capacity for resilience. Organizational research backs up this idea: The only measure that accurately predicts successful leadership for both men and women alike is whether one possesses the ability to cope with failure and grow from it — in other words, resilience.

Whether you are or will be a high achiever is determined by how you bounce back from your lows. If you let a short-term failure paralyze you with panic and self-doubt, or force you to retreat into your shell, then long-term success becomes harder to attain.

Because you are a woman who doesn't wait in line, you are going to come across a lot of naysayers. When you lose, you have to pull your chin up and resist the kind of negative self-talk that says you just aren't good enough. Criticism stings. Believe me, I know. But you have to stay strong. Don't let others' words or opinions define who you are or what you can do. Susan McPherson, the director of global marketing at Fenton Communications, says, "I try to imagine the conversation where failure is okay and it's only the beginning. So if I ask for a raise and

I get denied, then I might say, 'Well, okay, can you tell me some of the reasons?' And then, after I find out the reasons, I say, 'If I make progress on these things, can I come back to you?'" That's a smart and practical way to keep the ball rolling forward.

All of the women I admire and have interviewed have enormous reserves of strength. Each of them has experienced setbacks, but each also got up off the mat and kept fighting. Women in this generation have faced an economic environment rife with turmoil. We have been restructured, reorganized, and laid off more than any other generation.[13] But this has also taught us that we can weather any storm.

Katie Stanton is the head of international strategy at Twitter. Previously, she worked at Google, where she helped conceptualize, create, and launch Google Finance — it was her passion project. Then one day she got a call from her boss saying that she was going to be moved off the project because they needed someone with a fresh perspective. Katie was devastated.

Next, her colleagues asked her to join Google's OpenSocial team, which helps sites share their social data on the web. The project ultimately failed, but as Katie reflects, "It was because of this failure that I was able to reinvent myself." She left to work on new media strategies for then Senator Barack Obama's 2008 campaign. After the election, she became the first White House director of civic participation. Later, she helped the State Department integrate social media into diplomacy and development, which included using mobile technology to support disaster relief efforts in Haiti.

Katie's resilience and commitment to the long view of her career has served her well. In 2011, she was celebrated as a young female leader in several magazines, and by age forty-one she was already ranked on the *Forbes* list of the World's 100 Most Powerful Women. Developments that once seemed like professional setbacks ultimately led to extraordinary opportunities, and all because Katie knew how to roll with the punches.

To build resilience, make sure that you have a strong network of family and friends that you can lean on. Take the long view. See every failure as just one step toward success and not something that is insurmountable. Finally, nurture your self-confidence. And start today.

Beth Comstock, the chief marketing officer of GE, is one of the most influential women in business, but she spent the earlier part of her career doubting herself. Thinking about how she would have done things differently earlier in her career, she offers this advice to her younger self — and to the young women of today:

> I would tell my twenty-five-year-old self not to worry so much. I worried about the wrong things. As much as I think I went for it, there are things I didn't go for — mostly because of confidence. If I could bestow anything on a twenty-five-year-old, it would be the gift of confidence. I can't tell you how many times I've seen great women, great girls who have everything going for them, but they just have this fundamental sense of "I'm not confident." Your parents give it to you, your friends give it to you, but ultimately you [have to] give it to yourself.

2

Unapologetically Ambitious

W HEN I DECIDED TO RUN for Congress, the political establishment accused me of jumping the queue. I was chided for not following what the *New York Times* called the "traditional political protocol of running for a lower office first,"[1] accused of having "no credentials" by political consultants,[2] and cautioned by politically connected women and men to "build my career" with a smaller seat, a city council race, a state legislature race. After all, wrote the *Village Voice*, "none of the 17 city representatives in the House went straight there without prior public service, almost all elected first, like Maloney, to the assembly, state senate or city council."[3]

To be sure, the how-to manual for getting elected has long promoted the concept of "wait your turn" — especially in a place like New York, with its powerful political machine. Candidates are taught to prepare through a series of "smaller seats," so they can build up to play at the highest level. In part, it's about gaining experience as an elected official — but it's also about paying your dues to the establishment.

There is something to be said for investing as much time as you can in your profession and bolstering your skill set. It's important to build real relationships with key stakeholders and earn a reputation within an industry.

I get that. Yet I still can't help wondering: Is being an insider the best credential for bringing creative ideas and new initiatives to an industry in need of change? This certainly does not hold true for politics or any other profession. Some of the most successful people are those who have approached industry-specific problems from the point of view of an outsider, which freed them from long-held assumptions and allowed them to think outside the box. The world is a different place, and it's not uncommon for women to move laterally between professions instead of linearly up the ladder. Individuals who don't follow "the beaten path" often inject fresh perspectives into stale debates. We need new actors in every profession, with new ways of thinking and new relationships in their communities and beyond.

The Time Is Now

The "wait your turn" attitude can be especially pernicious toward women. "Know your place," "hide your ambition," and "wait your turn" are the kinds of messages that have been holding women back for much too long. By silently accepting these socials mores, we risk perpetuating the notion that our progress must be single file; that there can only be room in the arena for one strong woman at a time.

Too many women have been encouraged to overcommit to their preexisting activity or job, told to wait patiently for some arbitrary date, until they are "ready" to take the next step. But who's to tell us when we're ready? How can women make the best career choices for ourselves when we aren't encouraged to dream big about our futures?

The women I most admire, like Eleanor Roosevelt and Hillary Clinton, did not make history by patiently waiting in line. Instead of waiting to be picked, they embraced their ambition and picked themselves. Perhaps it wasn't immediate, but somewhere along their journey, they learned that waiting for opportunities to find them might mean coming up empty-handed.

These women understood the steep price of giving up their ambitions, not just for themselves but also for women as a whole. Institutional sexism and holding back have led women to earn less than our male peers, even though we work just as hard or harder. Playing it safe has led us into corners of boredom or depression at work because we have stuck with the safe and comfortable job instead of asking for a more challenging role with a bigger title. It's also led to a lot of student loan debt, advanced degrees gone to waste, and dreams deferred because we are simply afraid to admit that we want more.

Had I run for a lower seat, I would have been praised for my good behavior. My caution would have been interpreted as a demonstration of political acumen. I might have even won. But it also would have gone against everything I believed — everything I wanted to change. So I'm glad I ran in the race I did, however disappointing the outcome. Dreaming big also means that sometimes you have to fail before you can succeed.

If we want to close the ambition gap, we have to start taking risks. Apply for the job you're not qualified for! Women outnumber men in college enrollment and make up a greater percentage of the workforce, yet the number of women in leadership roles is a fraction of what it should be. The truth is, many women question their credentials and qualifications.

In 2011, 45.4 percent of all lawyers were women but only 19.5 percent of partners were women.[4] Moreover, the women who made partner were not involved in the same kinds of lucrative deals as their male counterparts: Among partners credited for more than $500,000 in business, a mere 16 percent were women.[5]

The same trends are revealed in medicine and business. In 2012, 34.3 percent of physicians were women, but more than 60 percent of those women physicians were in one of six specialties: internal medicine, pediatrics, family medicine, obstetrics/gynecology, psychiatry, and anesthesiology.[6] Female doctors continue to be found in the lower-paying, more care-oriented fields. In 2008 only three of more than a hundred chairs of surgery in the United States were filled by women, and there have been only six female chairs in history.[7]

In the business arena in 2011, women were only 14.1 percent of *Fortune* 500 executive officers and only 3.6 percent of *Fortune* 500 CEOs.[8] In academia, the achievement gap is similar. The National Center for Education reports that 84 percent of U.S. schoolteachers are female, but according to the American Council on Education only 26 percent of university presidents are female. Further, a mere 44 percent of women are tenured professors, reports the American Association for University Women.[9] Women are an overwhelming majority of all people working in education, but very few of them rise all the way to the highest ranks.

Lean In to Your Ambition

Merriam-Webster defines "ambition" as "an ardent desire for rank, fame, or power; desire to achieve a particular end." Is this kind of desire unnatural for women, or have we been conditioned by our culture to believe that it is somehow inappropriate and unseemly?

Some have argued the former — that women are simply less

ambitious by nature than men — suggesting that women rise, stall, and then vanish from the workplace by our own choice. I don't buy it.

The phenomenon of highly educated women leaving the workforce to become mothers, the so-called Opt-Out Revolution, was first described by Lisa Belkin in a 2003 *New York Times* story.[10] This turned out to be a fake phenomenon. According to a 2011 special report from McKinsey and Company titled *Unlocking the Full Potential of Women in the U.S. Economy*, diversity officers report "that motherhood, per se, rarely prompts a woman to stay put, downshift or look for work elsewhere."[11] Findings from a 2012 Gallup Poll support the claim: 75 percent of mothers with some form of a college degree work, while 48 percent of women without college degrees do.[12]

While it is true that some women opt out of their careers to have children, the "voluntary" nature of the decision is a matter of debate. Women are still getting signals from the workplace, society, and media that if you have a child and your financial situation permits, staying at home is the "right choice." As Tiffany Dufu, the chief leadership officer for Levo League, has argued, "All you have to be is a visibly pregnant woman to understand this. People only ask a pregnant woman if she is going to stay home with the child. It is never asked of the man. We live in a society where corporations are really set up for a 1950s male model of leadership and work, where a lot of time is spent on the job, and someone else is taking care of the children."[13]

Societal cues make women feel guilty about going back to work after childbirth. And yet women's requests for part-time or flexible work schedules are interpreted as symptoms of dulled ambition, when in fact they are quite the opposite. Instead of choosing to leave the workforce altogether, these women are looking for solutions that allow them to remain committed to the jobs and the children they love. They are trying to opt out of the unspoken ultimatum: work or family.[14] They want both. Fathers who are part of dual-earner families are also feeling greater work-life conflict as their partners spend greater time at work and their desire to be more involved with their children has increased.[15] It's no longer a women's issue; it's a family issue. Fathers also desire flexible work schedules to spend more time with their children.

Facebook chief operating officer Sheryl Sandberg offers another explanation for women's lack of professional advancement; she argues that to achieve gender parity and equity in the workforce:

> We need more women to lean into their careers and to be really dedicated to staying in the workforce. I think the achievement gap is caused by a lot of things. It's caused by institutional barriers and all kinds of stuff. But there's also a really big ambition gap. If you survey men and women in college today in this country, the men are more ambitious than the women. And until women are as ambitious as men, they're not going to achieve as much as men.[16]

Sheryl, whose stance on the ambition gap issue has been both applauded and widely criticized, points to studies showing that women are less ambitious than men when they graduate college and that this continues throughout their career. For example, a 2011 study by *More* magazine of five hundred college-educated women over the age of thirty-five found that 43 percent of respondents said they were less ambitious now than they were ten years ago.[17]

I don't think this study is asking the right question. I don't believe that women are innately less ambitious than men. Our society does not encourage women to take risks and embrace their real ambitions. If women have internalized the lesson that being ambitious is bad, then they may not answer the question honestly to begin with.[18]

The Next Generation

The Millennials demonstrate the ways in which society is already changing. Women like Lena Dunham and Tavi Gevinson are my "don't wait in line" generation. For them "patience is not seen as a virtue."[19]

Their generation is the most educated in U.S. history, and they are brimming with self-confidence. They have been told that they can do anything and have it all — career, family, and success — at the same time; become a mom *and* president of the United States. They have an insatiable hunger for challenges on the job. We can learn from these young women in how they demand responsibilities and opportunities.

Millennials expect to have both access and flexibility. Raised in a tech-savvy, transparent culture, where one tweet gets you access to Richard Branson and Lady Gaga, Millennials expect to have access to all levels of senior management and to share their ideas with them. They want to enjoy their work and have control over their lives.

Flextime is one policy implication for workplaces that would help keep women in the workforce and allow them to reach their ambitions. A 2008 study of twenty-five hundred people who were born after 1980 found that 85 percent of them wanted to spend 30 percent to 70 percent of their working time doing their job from home.[20] In a report done by the

Business and Professional Women's Foundation called *Gen Y Women in the Workplace*, Gen Y women were found to value self-management in their workplace environments. One Gen Y woman comments, "Society isn't 9am–5pm. I have the flexibility to work from home and I'm much more productive at home. I might run some errands during the day, but be online at 11pm. I'm still putting in a full day's work plus some, but I'm not confined to 9am–5pm."[21]

As *Forbes* blogger Julie Ruvolo explains, we don't feel limited the same way our mothers did:

> There has been a pivot to a more digital perspective, where women can work remotely and still be relevant and connected at the workplace. The digital paradigm has changed the concept of a ladder; there is now a digital fabric in the workplace. This fabric allows you to conceive of much bigger opportunities. Flexibility is important because it means that we are looking for career opportunities that give us the most room to expand. There is a paradigm shift happening and business cannot function the same way it used to.

Eight-Letter Word

I have talked to many different women about the so-called ambition gap. Women are not less ambitious than men; we've just been taught to suppress our goals or to doubt whether we can even achieve them. Writer and professor Anne-Marie Slaughter, who was the first woman to hold the position of director of policy planning in the U.S. State Department, told me, "It is extraordinary how deep taboos on women's ambition still run. Even to admit ambition is very hard. It still feels wrong to me. I grew up in the South. I definitely grew up in a place where girls were to be seen and not heard."

Recalling some of the "negative connotations that you get as a young girl growing up into womanhood," Beth Comstock, the CMO of General Electric, says: "Ambition, it's seen as being aggressive. Stating your mind is sometimes seen as being unpleasant. Trying to strive for a better way can sometimes be seen as being a bitch."

In her book *Necessary Dreams: Ambition in Women's Changing Lives*, Dr. Anna Fels argues that ambition has two "emotional engines": mastery and recognition. Part of being motivated to master a skill is the desire to be acknowledged for that achievement. And because women are socialized to put others' needs first, seeking public recognition can feel uncomfortable — even when we are very driven to achieve mastery. It is hard for us to publicly admit that we want the recognition too. As Fels has written, "The daily texture of women's lives from childhood on is infiltrated with microencounters in which quiet withdrawal, the ceding of available attention to others, is expected, particularly in the presence of men."[22]

When women deviate from these prescribed norms, society can be severe in its judgments. Whether it's *The Devil Wears Prada*, *The Iron Lady*, or *Black Swan*, we find caricatures of ambitious women portrayed as power hungry and constantly putting their personal ambitions before their family and personal relationships. The results of their ambition? The consequences are as dramatic as divorce, a lifetime of destitution and loneliness, and even death. The message is clear: Ambition is hazardous to a woman's well-being. Know and accept your place in life, or risk isolation by wearing your aspirations too proudly.

Throughout the 2008 presidential primary, Hillary Clinton

was berated for her ambition, which was often decried as "un-quenchable." I recall headline after headline — "Irrational Am-bition Is Hillary Clinton's Flaw." "Is Hillary Clinton Pathologi-cally Ambitious?" David Geffen, one of the biggest donors to the Democratic Party, stated, "I don't think that another incredibly polarizing figure, no matter how smart she is and no matter how ambitious she is — and God knows, is there anybody more ambi-tious than Hillary Clinton? — can bring the country together."[23] Or this one from Anne Applebaum in the *London Telegraph:* "the only real issue is Hillary Clinton's extraordinary, irrational, over-whelming ambition."[24] Her ambition was even used as a fund-raising tool to rally the troops by the GOP. The letter, which used the word "woman" five times, called her an "ambitious, ruthless, scheming, calculating, manipulating woman."[25]

I'll never forget the parody I read in the *Onion.* I'm ashamed to admit that when I first started reading it, it so accurately re-flected the prevailing attitude that I almost forgot it was meant to be satire. The article ended with this piece of advice:

> Ever heard of letting others take the lead, Sen. Clinton? If you're going to become the first woman in the Oval Office, you should start thinking about acting a little more ladylike.[26]

I have often confronted these attitudes myself as I try to fig-ure out my next political step. In November 2011, for example, the *New York Post* ran an article about my potential run for pub-lic advocate in 2013:

> Rising politico Reshma Saujani, who made a splash in 2010 when she challenged nine-term N.Y. Congresswoman Carolyn Ma-loney, still has her eye on public office. Sources say the 36-year-old Indian-American lawyer, who was crushed by Maloney in the

September congressional primary, has reached out to advisors about running for Public Advocate in 2013 if incumbent Bill De-Blasio runs for mayor. "She's very ambitious," a source said.[27]

"Ambitious." There's that word again.

If we let our ambition be hidden or thwarted, we will never accomplish our dreams. Now is the time to empower one another to embrace our ambition with pride, especially as younger generations are rising in the workforce and bringing new attitudes and expectations with them. Though they are few and far between, role models are out there. We need more young women in leadership positions so that young girls have role models to look up to. Look at Amy Poehler's character, Leslie Knope, on *Parks and Recreation*. She is unabashedly ambitious (she is always saying she wants to run for president) *and* she has a relationship *and* she has friends. *And* her boyfriend and friends and community love her for being clear about where she wants to go.

We are also redefining what it means for a woman to be ambitious today. Many of today's successful women define being ambitious as having a strong career, but not at the expense of family or mental sanity. That's different from the historical view that saw aspiration through the lens of career and professional success. Some of the most ambitious women I know are stay-at-home moms. They are the go-to women in their community: the ones who fight for the extra art or computer science programs in their kids' school. These women are the ones who are starting parent groups and bringing about real change on the ground. As far as I am concerned, they are just as aspiring as the women who want to be CEOs of companies. They are unstoppable and powerful in similar ways.

JUMP THE LINE

Own Your Ambition

For too long, women have accepted the message that ambition is a negative quality; that it means that we are selfish, egotistical, manipulative, or power hungry. This leads us to deny or minimize our professional accomplishments and compromise our shot at greater responsibilities, bigger stages, and higher salaries. Meanwhile, men embrace ambition as a necessary trait for success. They demand more for themselves. It's time for women to do the same.

Don't apologize for being proud of meeting your professional goals or for killing it at that big presentation in front of your company's executive board or for getting that promotion you worked your ass off for. Celebrate your victories, large and small. After the episode with the *New York Post*, I made shirts for the holidays with the word "ambition" on the front with little red devil horns. On the back I printed the quote, "'She's very ambitious,' a source said." Let's stop running from the label and, instead, own it.

Find Your Dharma

Today, boys and girls are both being raised to believe they can accomplish anything they set their minds to. That's good; we shouldn't settle for anything less. And yet this feeling of "I can do anything" has led some women to wander. I meet countless young women who tell me that they want to do everything — with the unfortunate result that they can't focus on anything. One of my mentees wants to be a writer, start her own fashion line, and be a foreign policy correspondent. As one Millennial writes in her blog:

> Now, I'm at the start of a career, looking at what I've done so far. Graduating with two majors in four years, with honors and a Summa status. Leaving college and getting an internship with a *Fortune* 500 company and parlaying that into a full-time gig at a Franchise 500 company, all while attending grad school full time and commuting insane distances every day for several years. Sure, these things are great, and I'm proud of my accomplishments, but I can't help knowing that even now, I want more.
>
>   I still want to do it all.[28]

First things first: Define what you want to achieve. If part of fulfilling your ambition is mastering a skill, you need to spend the time to figure out what you want to do with your life. Invest in yourself and spend the time to take stock of your skills and passions. Self-reflection and introspection are a necessary part of uncovering your dharma, your mission in life.

I do not mean to suggest you need to have a rigid plan. But you need to understand what moves you, what makes you happy, where you feel like your talents can make an impact. As Joanna Barsh, Susie Cranston, and Geoffrey Lewis, the authors of *How Remarkable Women Lead*, state, a job becomes your calling when "it draws on your core strengths, engages you fully, and inspires you through a higher purpose."[29]

Here is a practical step you can take:

To help find your dharma, write a personal mission statement. If you don't know what specific job you want in ten years, then think about your mission statement in broad-brush terms. Think about the words you want to reflect your life. Maybe it will be in public service or as a change agent, or perhaps yours is more along the lines of work-life balance or becoming financially independent.

By identifying your dharma, you will make your ambition sacred. You will prioritize your goals, and you will be less willing to give them up.

Be Loud, Be Proud

Speak up. Visibility begets access, and access begets opportunity. Take responsibility for making sure that people know who you are and the contributions you make.

Don't assume that just because you're good, the people who matter will notice. Tiffany Dufu explains, "Performance matters, but what also matters is making sure that you're visible, making sure that you've aligned yourself with the right people, making sure that you've got the plum assignment, and really understanding that all that extracurricular activity stuff that you thought wasn't really a part of your job, that actually *is* your job."

So go ahead and take a seat at the table. If there aren't enough seats, pull up a chair. Challenge yourself to speak up in every meeting. As Betsy Morgan, former CEO of the Huffington Post, puts it, "You *have* to participate. If you've been invited to a meeting, if you've been invited to collaborate on something, if you've been included in something, you have to participate."

Get comfortable being your own PR agent. Yes, I'm telling you to toot your own horn. It's okay. Twitter, LinkedIn, Facebook, and other social media tools allow you to do this very easily. Make a monthly list of accomplishments and keep a "brag bag" — a file of all the great things you have done: articles you have written, compliments you have received from supervisors or colleagues, awards that you have won. Support your friends and they'll support your causes, events, and accomplishments too. Be a cheerleader on social media. When you are at an event or networking, use your accomplishments to introduce yourself properly and feel comfortable talking about how badass you are.

And what about all those Top twenty under twenty, thirty under thirty, or forty under forty lists? Plenty of men nominate themselves and have their friends and family do the same thing. You can too. Make a list of the top recognitions that would be helpful for you in your field and ask people to put your name forward. Don't be embarrassed. If you think you deserve the honor, your friends and colleagues probably will too. I participate on a listserv of women in technology and new media called Change the Ratio started by my friend Rachel Sklar. Every week a member of the group will reach out and ask the community to nominate her for an award or a list that is relevant in her field. Once a person takes the initiative of filling out the form, we all nominate her.

So get out there! Young women today have boundless energy and excitement. Make sure you use this energy not only within your workplace but also in the outside world. Go to conferences, meet as many people as you can, and gain outside perspectives. By exposing yourself to lots of interesting people and professions, you may discover a career path you never knew existed.

Create a Personal Board of Directors

Several women I know, including eBay's marketing chief Richelle Parham, have what they call a personal board of directors. How do you create one? First, you need to write a mission statement that reflects the goals you want to achieve over the next two to five years. Then identify five to seven people you'd like to sit on your advisory board. This must be a group of people you trust to give honest feedback on everything that matters to you. If part of your personal mission is to have a baby in the next two years, you want to make sure your board includes personal friends as well as professional colleagues.

Remember, A players surround themselves with A players. Pick people who are smarter than you and whose experience and knowledge are complementary. Convene your board once a year. Set aside at least half a day to go over your mission statement. See which goals you have made, which ones you have missed, and which ones you should change.

Your personal board doesn't have to be this formal. You can also have a group of people that you informally convene to help you reach your goals. The point is you need to organize people in your life whom you can rely on for honest, unflinching advice, who will hold you accountable for your goals, and who are committed to helping you be the best you can be.

3

Don't Worry If They Don't Like You

BY JANUARY 2010, I was officially running in the Democratic primary in New York's Fourteenth District. One Saturday, I appeared on Fox News, paired with two extremely combative male co-panelists. They were yelling and ranting, barely letting each other finish their sentences before jumping in to interrupt. I had plenty of ideas, but I patiently, politely waited my turn — until the producer started screaming into my earpiece, "Get into the fight!"

"What?" I thought. I wanted people to see me as a forceful leader, but I wanted them to like me too. I wasn't going to be rude and interrupt. I was being nice.

What I didn't realize was that from the viewers' perspective, my deference made me look weak. To them, I wasn't being nice. I was being walked all over.

After the interview, I thought I had learned my lesson. Be as aggressive as the guys. Don't wait to be asked, just speak your mind. Nobody wants to see you shrink from a fight.

That was the mentality I brought to a conversation just over a year later, in early 2011. After I lost the primaries, I started making the rounds, speaking to New York's top political consultants about what I should do next. I was excited to secure an appointment with an influential pollster. He was regarded as one of the best and brightest minds in the business. This pollster had discouraged me from running for Congress in 2010, but since I wasn't running against an incumbent this time, I thought he would be more open to my ideas for running for New York City's public advocate in 2013.

As I entered his office, he was wearing his headset and was fielding two conversations simultaneously. Everything about him signified intensity, brashness, and drive.

I told him that I wanted to run for public advocate, but he immediately cut me off.

"Even if you saved New York City from a terrorist attack, you couldn't win this race." He shook his head emphatically.

I pressed on. He interrupted again, waving his hand dismissively in the air. "Look, Reshma," he said. "You're too aggressive. You need to tone it down. Take Congresswoman X. I'll tell you why she's a successful fundraiser. Before she asks a guy for a check, she gives him a smile. She butters him up. And *then* she goes in for the wallet." He paused. "You could learn something from her."

The pollster then offered to introduce me to a few key influencers in the city, but he wanted to coach me first. He had to make sure I amped up the sugar and toned down the spice.

"Thanks but no thanks," I thought. I'd heard enough. I gathered my things and left.

But I left confused. In the Fox interview, I'd been told I wasn't tough enough. Now I was being told I was too tough. What was the Goldilocks formula? Was I too passive? Or was I too aggressive? And if I was aggressive, then so what? When men act tough, they aren't punished; they're praised. Why should it be different for women? And whatever happened to just being yourself?

Throughout our lives, women are taught to be deferential, to speak quietly, to avoid rocking the boat. We are taught to sit with our legs crossed and our hands neatly folded in our laps. Those of us who refuse to be submissive are criticized for our sass. Sometimes we are even criticized by other women who themselves have been reprimanded for being too outspoken or aggressive. What's most infuriating to me is that over time, as women are repeatedly admonished for being aggressive, we start repressing the impulse to stand up for ourselves.

The pressure starts when we're young. From a very early age, little girls are socialized to be sweet. When a girl takes a toy from someone, pulls another child's hair, or talks back, she is told to "be good" or "be a nice girl." Girls respond to criticism by being quiet; boys act out even more. They grab more toys, pull tighter, and get louder.

The Baby Boomers have chipped away at some gender stereotypes. Take, for example, the Free to Be You and Me Foundation, a division of the Ms. Foundation for Women, started by Pat Carbine, Letty Cottin Pogrebin, Gloria Steinem, and Marlo Thomas. The campaign began as an album and illustrated book that sought to empower children by teaching them that you can be anything regardless if you are a boy or a girl.[1] Another example is the Barbie Liberation Army, which challenges Barbie's image by hacking the voice boxes on Barbies and G.I. Joes and switching the dolls' gendered voice message.[2] Yet there's no doubt that everyone from advertisers to toy makers to entertainment companies still manufacture products that perpetuate traditional constructions of gender, constructions that prize "ladylike" qualities in girls.

Consider, for example, the $4 billion Disney Princess empire. Disney packages and sells dolls, dresses, and other memorabilia based on the female heroines from its animated feature-

length films. In 2011, Disney unveiled plans for a Princess Sofia
the First, a young girl who, due to unforeseen circumstances
(Sofia is a "commoner" whose mother marries a king), becomes
a princess. Without an ounce of irony, Disney has been boasting
about this royal who keeps it real. According to its press release,
"Although Sofia will have plenty of pretty dresses and sparkly
shoes, our stories will show Sofia, and our viewers, that what
makes a real princess is what's inside, not what's outside. That
the inner character of kindness, generosity, loyalty, honesty and
grace make you special, not the dress you wear."[3]

Kindness. Loyalty. Grace.

How about intelligence? Guts? Strength?

No, Disney seems hell-bent on teaching yet another generation to worship a sweet little girl in a pretty dress.

But Disney is hardly the only company to market a mind-
boggling array of pink products to little girls. A movie called
Barbie: Princess Charm School, aired on the children's network
Nick Jr., offers five tips to "bring the princess in every girl to
life."[4]

For example, Lesson #2: "Set a table — Every princess needs
to know how to set a perfect princess table for friends and
family."

Or Lesson #5: "How to write a thank-you note — When a
princess receives a gift, she should use lovely stationery and
write a thank-you note right away."

Don't get me wrong: I'm a fan of good manners, and I agree
they should be taught. But why just to girls? Why are princes
groomed to rule the castle, while princesses are schooled to set
the table?

What our culture teaches girls from a very young age is that
it's important to be liked and, above all, to accommodate others.

We take those messages with us into the working world. We

want to be polite, so we wait to be called on. We don't want to come off as too opinionated, so we qualify our opinions and speak in questions instead of statements. We ask for permission to pursue new ideas, instead of trusting our own instincts and forging ahead. And we struggle to make people aware of our accomplishments because we fear coming off as arrogant.

As Kate White, author of *Why Good Girls Don't Get Ahead ... but Gutsy Girls Do*, writes, girls hear the message that "one of the most important jobs a female has is considering and taking care of others' needs, and in the process that often involves putting her own needs aside."[5]

Even when we have earned opportunities ourselves, we think we have to be grateful to others. Katie Stanton, the head of international strategy at Twitter, was recently invited to be on a board of another company. She says, "I was asked to meet with one of the members and have coffee with the CEO. When they asked whether I would sit on their board, I told them how flattered I was that they would ask me. Later, when I told a recruiter friend about my reaction, she got mad at me for telling the CEO how grateful I was for the opportunity. She thought I should say of course and boast about why I am qualified. I felt like that was obnoxious."

Women tend to do many other self-defeating things in our quest for likability—apologizing, qualifying, taking the back bench, going the extra mile but taking no credit. And it would be one thing if being likable actually helped us advance in the workplace. But it doesn't! Our bosses come to see us as less eager or hardworking than our male colleagues, simply because we are too modest to blow our own horns. How many times have you sweated blood over a team project, only to see a guy swipe all the credit?

What we fail to understand is that there is a difference between being liked and being respected—in life and in the working world. Too often, the things we do to be liked make us seem weak instead of strong. We behave like good girls and find ourselves competing against men who have been taught to be aggressive, assertive, and confident. If those are the qualities that get recognized and rewarded professionally, then women need to cultivate them too.

But receiving the recognition and advancement we deserve is more complicated than that, because women face a catch-22 in the workplace. We're *expected* to be likable—yet it's hard for us to be likable and ambitious at the same time.

Kathryn Minshew, the founder of the Muse website, recalls an experience that illustrates this well. "My mom was always worried about girls getting a bad reputation, so she taught me to be demure," says Kathryn. "She taught me, if you can't say something nice don't say anything at all. My brother was taught to break things, push boundaries, and thump his chest. I was taught that being self-promotional was bad, that I shouldn't be arrogant. I was taught to put others before myself."

By the time Kathryn got her first job at the top consulting firm McKinsey and Company, she had already been programmed to fear being disliked and to adopt a more deferential style of communication. In her mind, this decision was validated by her initial experience at the firm, where she quickly learned that people did not think highly of aggressive women.

For example, she heard many people call one of the few female partners in the office a bitch. Kathryn says that this particular female partner was tough but far less aggressive than the male partners.

Kathryn picked up on the signals and behaved in the opposite way. She was diligent, dedicated, and demure, trusting that her work ethic would be noticed by her superiors. After meetings, she would even help the secretary clear the coffee cups, thinking that they would appreciate her team-playing attitude. She stopped, however, when her male supervisor told her it was preventing her from being taken seriously.

I want to be clear: Being liked is not a bad thing. Many of the qualities women embrace are truly valuable. We need leaders who are more inclusive and thoughtful. Moreover, women aren't the only ones who care about being liked. Research shows that likability can be beneficial for followers and leaders of both sexes.[6] If a colleague or employee likes you, he or she is more likely to follow your instructions. Naturally, if people don't like you, you will have more difficulty with personal relationships at work.

But the *desire* to be liked has a critical relationship to power — and the deck is already stacked in men's favor. Many women face a double bind since likability is important to get ahead, but the very traits that make one likable — modesty, humility — are not the ones that lead to raises and promotions. Professional recognition flows from stereotypically masculine behaviors such as self-confidence, assertiveness, and asking directly for what you want. As one study by the research organization Catalyst points out, "To the extent that people still equate stereotypically masculine behaviors and traits with effective leadership, men are cast as 'natural leaders,' while women constantly must prove that they can lead."[7]

When it comes to the qualities we expect in a leader, women are held to different standards. Serious female leaders are expected to be sober and businesslike, never displaying a fun side; yet if we are too serious, like the McKinsey partner Kathryn talked about, then we are called bitches, ice queens, or worse.

Behavior seen as confident in men is characterized as pushy in women — a reality Facebook chief operating officer Sheryl

Sandberg acknowledged at the 2012 World Economic Forum, when she asked the audience, "Anyone at Davos who as a girl was called bossy? If you got to Davos you were that. I was."[8]

Navigating these complex waters can be stressful and confusing. According to Rachel Simmons, author of *The Curse of the Good Girl*: "This generation has had it ingrained in them that they must thrive within a 'yes, but' framework: Yes, be a go-getter, but don't come on too strong. Yes, accomplish, but don't brag about it. The result is that young women hold themselves back, saying, 'I shouldn't say this, ask for this, do this — it will make me unlikable, a bitch, or an outcast.'"[9]

There has also been rigorous research done on the financial downside to being tough. A Harvard study found that women who demand higher starting salaries are perceived as "less nice" and thus less likely to be hired.[10] Men are four times more likely than women to negotiate their first salary because they don't fear coming off as aggressive or unlikable. Twenty percent of adult women — some 22 million — say that they never negotiate at all.[11] The compounding effect of this is enormous. By failing to negotiate your first salary, you stand to lose more than $500,000 by the age of sixty.[12]

Settling for less than we are worth tends to hamstring women throughout our careers. Women ask for raises and promotions 85 percent less often than their male counterparts do, and when they do ask, they ask for 30 percent less.[13] This contributes to an enormous pay gap. As of 2008, women aged twenty-one to thirty earn 89 percent of what men earn.[14] Contrary to the popular belief that the reason for this pay gap is women who opt out of the workforce for motherhood, research shows that "a decade out of college, full-time working women who *haven't* had children still make 77 cents on the male dollar."[15]

This inability to ask doesn't just harm salary negotiations; it also hurts women who are trying to start their own companies. Many of the female entrepreneurs I interviewed said it took a while for them to feel comfortable asking investors for money. Kathryn Minshew said, "I would be at a meeting with a potential investor, and when the meeting ended, I would say, 'Great, I will keep you posted,' instead of directly asking the question I went there to ask: 'Will you invest in my company?' I had to force myself to practice asking, but it was imperative that I did."

In a similar vein, studies have shown that women are less likely to receive venture capital funding: A mere 4 to 9 percent of all venture capital funding goes to women.[16] Of course, nothing is black and white. The percentage of women's businesses that receive funding is due to more than just gender. Studies cite that the types of businesses that women usually start — lifestyle and home-based enterprises — do not often meet criteria for VC funding. One of the reasons for that may be that most VCs are male and cannot relate to their businesses.

Can women be appreciated for both their leadership and interpersonal style? Do we have to choose between wanting to be liked and owning our success?

The first step is acknowledging our unconscious biases and working to proactively change our behavior. The solution starts with us. We need to recognize our own unconscious decisions to downplay our merits and accomplishments.

It's natural to want to walk into a boardroom, an investor meeting, or a networking event and have everyone smile at you. But at the end of the day, your sense of self-worth should not depend on other people's feelings about you. Many women have told me, "I could never run for office because I don't know how I would handle all those awful things people say in the comment section of a blog." The reality is that no matter how hard you try, some people simply will not like you. That's okay.

Remind yourself that sometimes friction is necessary to generate heat and light. Take a page from men's playbook and try to depersonalize the situation. Ask yourself: Do your critics dislike you, or do they dislike your ideas?

We can't let the desire to be liked get in the way of doing the right thing and making the tough calls — especially when we're the ones in charge. If you're too focused on being liked, you may get caught up in indecision, refusing to make the choices that might be unpopular among the group. Worse, you could make the wrong decision because you're thinking more about not rocking the boat, not angering anyone, than you are about doing the right thing. No matter what others say and think, you will do your career a far better service by doing the best job you can — and that means sometimes making difficult and even unpopular decisions. In the end, integrity is what will earn respect.

Changing our own behavior still isn't enough. We also need to question other people's perceptions and judgments about women in power. When you hear someone call a female boss a bitch, or you hear someone question a woman's aggression, don't sit there silently. Push back. Press them on why they feel that way and what that woman has done to deserve the insult. We all need to do our part to help dispel stereotypes that are negative or harmful to women.

JUMP THE LINE

Take Credit, Collaborate, and Be the Boss —
All at the Same Time

There is no reward for being bashful. When your boss compliments you on acing an important client meeting or delivering a product that exceeds expectations, don't shirk the credit. Take credit where credit is due. There is a way to do this gracefully and while bringing other people along with you. For example, you could respond to praise by saying, "Thanks. My team and I worked hard on this project and spent a lot of late nights at the office." And if your boss doesn't ask, tell him or her about your accomplishments anyway. It pays to speak up. A recent Catalyst study found that "when women were more proactive in making their achievements visible they advanced further, were more satisfied with their careers, and had greater compensation growth than women who were less focused on calling attention to their successes."[17]

Tough girls believe in building relationships with others. That doesn't mean downplaying your authority or trying to be a friend instead of the boss. It means working hard to strike a balance between taking ownership over your own talent, skills, and work product and being inclusive and complimentary of your team.

Through it all, whether you are a woman or a man, never burn bridges — the world is small. My mentor, A. Leon Higginbotham Jr., would always tell me that you have to treat everyone with respect. It is a lesson that I have followed my entire career.

Own Aggressive

Owning aggressive means you don't wait to be called on. Speak up when you have something to say, and don't be afraid to argue passionately for your position. If you won't defend it, who will?

I learned this lesson after the interview on Fox News. Now when I go on a TV interview or have a public speaking event, I focus on what's most important — the message I want to convey. I've learned to stop undermining my own authority with verbal softeners, such as "You probably have already thought of this, but . . ." or "I might be wrong, but . . ." I also watch out for how many times I say the words "like" and "um." Using the word "like" in every other sentence sends a signal that we are not confident about our point of view.

Being well liked is not the most important value; being effective is. And sometimes, you may just have to piss people off in the process of getting things done.

Similarly, as a person in a position of authority, don't be afraid to delegate. It isn't the smartest use of your time to try to do everything yourself. Part of being a leader means taking charge of your team and assigning tasks. It also means getting rid of the anxiety that you don't want to burden someone else.

This is not a call for a generation of mean girls — it's a call for an army of confident women who together can serve as a force for change. The key to success lies in finding the balance between what are traditionally thought of as masculine and feminine traits — competence and likability. We need to teach men to be more inclusive in their leadership styles and encourage women to maintain their inclusive style while embracing their more assertive side.

Ask for Negative Feedback

I have a pretty high tolerance for criticism. Some of it has to do with how I was raised. When I won an award or got a top grade, my father never applauded me. I could have done better, and who was to say I wouldn't win the next contest or excel on the next test? When I stumbled, he never told me that it was okay. That's still true now: The day after my election, instead of sending me a care package, my father sent me an email with the subject line "The Top Ten Things You Did Wrong." Sometime later, we were at the Lincoln Memorial together and I remarked that Abraham Lincoln lost seven elections. Dad looked at me and said, "That was over a hundred years ago; today you can win the first time." What I took away from my father's approach to failure is that we have to get up when we fall, learn from our mistakes, and try to do better next time.

In Chapter 2, I talked about how important it is to have the confidence to go after your dreams. Once you are truly confident, you can be fearless about asking for feedback, because criticism won't rip at your foundation; it will make you even better at what you already know you can do. Ask the people you work with on a daily basis for feedback about your work performance. If you are applying to school, ask your friends to review your application or personal statement.

Every time I finish a speech, I ask my staff to rate me from 1 to 10. I don't ask for praise; I tell them I want to know what I can do better. I taught myself not to take their criticism personally. What they have to say is important to me because I want to improve my skills and evolve as a public speaker.

Many of the women I interviewed had colleagues or bosses who were able to give them honest feedback. At first they found it tough to take the criticism. It's understandable to feel defensive and tense, but we have to let go of this in order to evolve.

My father wrote me a letter the day after my wedding, saying that he was happy to see so many of my friends standing up giving speeches during the reception, supporting and encouraging my political aspirations. He wrote, "I observed that you had several people saying yes you can do it and willing to support you. That is just great! However, you may need to find and listen to at least one person who can be critical of you so you can properly align your path with your goals effectively." Dad!

If there's one thing I've learned from my father's toughness, it's that honest feedback about mistakes and failures leads to growth. It takes a tremendous amount of strength to subject yourself to public scrutiny. Our deepest instincts run counter to asking for outright rejection. But you must do it. You will face criticism in the future. People will use it to break your will and dent your dedication. By soliciting negative feedback on your own, you can learn how to control your reactions, how not to take it personally, and how to keep your anger in check. You'll be better equipped to respond effectively because you won't feel as bruised emotionally.

It's equally important to learn how to *give* constructive criticism. If a girlfriend applies for a job and doesn't get it, go through her application with her and help her figure out where she can make improvements. If you mentor or sponsor a young woman, commit to giving her honest feedback. It is the only way she will grow and develop.

If You Don't Ask, You Don't Get

Ask for what you want. Whether it's a job, a raise, or for someone to invest in your idea. You won't get unless you ask. Ty Stiklorius is partner of the Artists Organization, a management company that includes clients such as John Legend and Soundgarden. Ty also serves on the board of Women's Campaign International, an organization that trains local leaders to give them the leadership skills they need to advocate for change in their communities. She has many thoughts on the importance of asking and believes we have to learn how to express our discomfort in certain things so that we get what we want. "I see these *young* girls, like three-year-olds, four-year-olds, up to ten or eleven or twelve, being just fucking ballsy. They're expressive . . . they're asking for what they need. They're on the playground, and then something shifts where it becomes about 'Oh no, I must be likable, feminine, kissable,'" she says. "And if you learn this sort of gentleness at a young age, by the time you get to the workplace it could be hard to remember your ten-year-old kick-ass, kickball girl self. Women need to channel that ballsy young girl and not be afraid to ask for what you need and express what you need."

Women often do a great job negotiating or asking on behalf of their employers, or on behalf of someone else, but when it comes to ourselves, many of us are horrible at negotiating for what we want. How many times have you been afraid to ask for a raise, an investment in your company, or the title change that you know you deserve? Sometimes we don't ask because we think it's not necessary and that someone will notice how hard we are working and just reward us. Sometimes we don't want to be seen as greedy. Sometimes we just listen to the "wait till you earn it" advice. Sometimes we just want our boss to like us.

Asking for more is complicated and may not always result in success. But we cannot change the paradigm until more of us start asking.

The bottom line is that if you don't ask for the opportunity, you don't get it. Your boss will say she didn't know about your aspirations. Be strategic about what you ask for and figure out what strengths you can leverage. Do your research. Determine what you are worth, bring in evidence and facts — whether it's about average salaries in a given industry or how much a particular investor tends to offer to start-up companies.

Don't limit yourself to asking other women about their experience; chances are you are both underpaid. Instead, survey the market. Know the industry standard, and know where you rank within it. Educate yourself on what the top earners make. Then make a list of everything you have done, and practice emphasizing your achievements. Rehearse selling yourself. Ask directly for what you want. And after you're done, wait for your boss to respond. Don't try to fill the silence. Don't add the line you may be dying to say: "I am sorry I had to ask, I hope I am not putting you in a hard spot."

Most important, start to enjoy the art of negotiation.

Most women I know, myself included, hate talking about money. We have to change our attitudes, otherwise there will always be pay inequity between men and women. When we fail to negotiate, all we are doing is showing our bosses that we think we are less worthy or successful than a man does who has done the same work. That's why I began this book by talking about building your confidence. That is step number one in knowing your value; the next step is demanding that you be paid or invested in accordingly.

As Whitney Johnson, founding partner of Rose Park Advisors, an investment firm, and author of *Dare, Dream, Do*, says:

> Ask for what you want. You may not get it, but you won't leave empty-handed. At the very least, you'll get information. You put an ask on the table, an opening request; your employer or partners or board counters with a bid. If the ask and the bid are close, you know something. If they aren't close, will the bidders negotiate? You'll know something else.[18]

To demand your place at the table, educate yourself so you can face any conversation with a clear mind and a clear voice. Know your goal and stick to it by remaining levelheaded and attentive.

Approach the table ready to negotiate and to actively seek an outcome. Practice on your own time. Forget about your fears by visualizing positive outcomes for your negotiations. Focus on the impacts of your action. Envision a clear, well-defined outcome and then say it out loud.

4

Follow Your Bliss

IN JANUARY 2009, I was thirty-four and the deputy chief operating officer of a public hedge fund called Fortress Investment Group. As one of the few senior women at the firm, I had enormous responsibilities and was gaining valuable management skills. I was moving up swiftly within the corporate hierarchy. I was finally worrying less about whether I would be able to pay off my student loans or help my parents with their mortgage.

And yet, despite these outward trappings of success, I felt increasingly lost.

For almost as long as I could remember, I had wanted to serve my country. But over the years, the decisions I'd made had been pushing me in another direction. I had pursued corporate work to pay my student loans and to reassure my immigrant parents that their sacrifices had not been in vain. In addition, I was trying to put myself on firm financial footing and to build the funding foundation I knew a candidate needed to run.

Somehow, without realizing it, the money part had overtaken the public service dream. And now here I was, on a fast track, barreling in the wrong direction.

In the wake of the financial crisis, it became clear to me

where my head and heart really lay. Instead of helping For-tress rebuild, I wanted to help people who had lost their jobs and homes, people whose lives had been upended. My work in finance gave me a firsthand view of what had gone wrong and powerful knowledge about what laws and regulations needed to be written to prevent another crisis. That's what I felt passion-ately about. That's what I wanted to be a part of. But how could I walk away from my growing role within the firm?

Terrified as I was of taking the leap, the alternative seemed equally horrifying.

I didn't want to wake up one day and realize my dreams had passed me by. I thought back to myself as a little girl, taping that *U.S. News and World Report* of the top law schools to the fridge.

My big break — literally — came in January 2009 when I tore my ACL in a ski accident. Confined to my couch for three months, I had plenty of time for focused thinking, and reexam-ining and reprioritizing my own life. I couldn't run. I couldn't read because the painkillers made my brain feel a little fuzzy. I couldn't work. I had plenty of time to think about what I was doing with my life and why I wasn't leading the professional life I wanted to lead.

When I was finally able to go back to work, I was ready to make a change.

I walked into my boss's office and quit, and left most of my bonus, and all of my burdens, behind.

Changing Lanes

Too many educated, successful, high-achieving women aren't finding themselves where they want to be. But sometimes the problem isn't that we're too willing to wait in line. The problem is that we're in the *wrong* line. Instead of jumping the queue, we need to get out of the queue altogether and find a better avenue to realize our talents and aspirations.

Why do so many women find it hard to get up and move on to something better? Here are three main reasons women find it difficult to make a change.

First, we feel like leaving is admitting defeat — and we don't like admitting defeat to our friends, family, and colleagues. We think they will be disappointed with us and we are afraid of what they will say. We play out their potential questions, their likely criticisms, their concerns: "Are you crazy, who quits in this economy?" or "How will you support yourself?" or "Did you get another job?" And we hate the thought of falling short in their eyes. Who cheers for the woman who gives up?

Certainly, my fear of what others would say was a major reason I continued working in law and finance even though I was miserable. In particular, and perhaps especially as a daughter of immigrants, I didn't want to let my family down.

I have spoken to many daughters of immigrants who have felt the same way, so there's certainly a cultural element to this fear. We have financial and emotional obligations to our family that make it hard for us to quit. We feel like our parents worked so hard to help us get an education that it would be selfish not to take the highest-paying job we can find. Although children are almost always eager to make their parents proud, second-generation children of immigrants may feel a special pressure to conform to traditional notions of success.

Second, when we hate our jobs, we think about all the time and effort we have already invested in our current situation, time and effort we have wasted being miserable — if we leave, it will all have been for nothing, an investment with no gain. That time and effort — from the weekend conference we were forced to attend to the professional training we suffered through—is the definition of sunk costs. No, we cannot get those days back, but they should not have any bearing on our future decisions. Obsessing over those costs is actually measuring the wrong things. It's calculating how much we'll have lost if we leave and if things get better. But what about the cost of all of the missed opportunities, and to our own happiness, if we stay where we are?

Third, we talk ourselves into believing that things will change. We stick it out because we think things will get better even though all signs point to the fact that it won't. So we grit our teeth and doggedly, dutifully plug away, even when it feels like we're beating our head against wall.

Of course, sometimes a job—any job—is a necessary way to pay the bills. I won't devalue the importance of stability. But sticking with a job you hate is ultimately counterproductive, as it will be harder for you to do well and harder to advance. When you are doing what you love, the money and stability will follow. Getting out of the wrong line and into the right one can be scary, but changing course can change your life for the better.

How do you know when it's time to go? What are the signs to watch out for?

The first major sign is losing passion for your work or realizing that you weren't passionate about your job in the first place. Many of us are not satisfied with just any job; we are looking for our calling. In fact, in a study done by the American Business Collaboration for Quality Dependent Care, women cited "finding meaning" in their work as the most important factor in choosing a job and staying with it, outside of salary.[1] Some data suggests that women might even be willing to trade off higher pay in order to have a job they find fulfilling.[2]

This makes sense. When you have passion and purpose, it is more likely that you will ride and conquer what author Seth Godin describes as the "Dip." In his book of the same name, he defines the Dip as the stretch of time between starting a job and mastering that job. During this time, you feel like you want to quit; every task feels challenging and difficult. Godin argues that if you are in the job you are meant to be in, you will "lean into the Dip" — meaning, embrace it — you will have a higher morale and you will be more effective during that time period.[3] If you don't feel that passion, that sense of purpose that propels you to weather the challenges that come with mastering something new, it could be a sign that the job is not the right fit for you.

The second sign that it's time to leave is if you start to realize that the financial, emotional, and physical costs of your job just aren't worth it. As Stephanie Harbour says:

> In the younger generation right now, there's this kind of workaholic mentality where you're burning out at a pretty young age. You're not burning out when you're fifty and kind of inching your way toward retirement. You're burning out when you're twenty-nine. That you've been working for eight years and you are just absolutely destroyed and then just quit and travel the world for two years. You know, I have a . . . male friend who was in banking who walked away. Walked away. Went and climbed Kilimanjaro and then moved to Brazil. He was completely burned out. The point is, careers are long and we have to pace ourselves.

We have to consider the cost of "burnout." Unhappiness at your job can impact your health. According to the American Psychological Association, job burnout can lead to "depression, anxiety, and physical illness. Drugs or alcohol are often a problem."[4] The APA also finds that after an extended period of time burnout becomes serious, causing physical and mental breakdowns, which could lead to risks as grave as suicide, stroke, or heart attack.

The third sign it is time to quit is if you think that no matter how hard you work, you won't ever be better than mediocre at your job. It may be that the job itself isn't a good fit for your skill set — but more likely, it's that your heart isn't in it. For example, I am a super type A person, but over the decade I spent working in law and finance, I was okay playing a B game. That alone should have been a huge wake-up call to me that I was in the wrong line.

The fourth sign that it's time to leave your job is if you are intellectually stagnating. If you're not being challenged and stimulated, you need to move on. That doesn't mean that every task has to be sexy and exciting. Especially when you are just starting out, you may have to send out a fax and lick some envelopes, or do other seemingly mindless tasks. I believe that no work should be beneath you and being a team player is important. But overall, your job should be challenging. You should be learning. You should be getting your share of responsibility and recognition.

This kind of learning plateau is important to recognize. "I left Facebook because I believe when you stop learning it's time to leave," says Randi Zuckerberg, the former CMO of Facebook. "You stay at a career when you are learning more than you are giving. There is this fine balance, between learning and giving back, and as soon as the balance shifts and you are not learning anymore is when you have to leave. It is exactly when the job gets comfortable that it is most important to leave, and it's scary as shit."

A word of caution: Just as you should recognize when it's time to go, whenever you are thinking about leaving a job or career, make sure it's for the right reasons.

In part, that means taking both the short and long view. As women, we want to come to work every day and be happy, whereas men will deal with some short-term discomfort for long-term financial gain. In fact, a study done by Sally Helgesen and Julie Johnson in *The Female Vision* demonstrates that women value their work depending on their daily experiences, while men value work on the basis of what it might lead to in the future.[5] Of course, making this mind-set change isn't always easy, especially during the moments when your job is particularly rough.

It's important to understand that. You need to stop and ask yourself: Is your dissatisfaction a reaction to short-term circumstances, or is it going to prove chronic? Has your working life become a disaster, or are you merely in the Dip?

Mika Brzezinski, the cohost of MSNBC's *Morning Joe*, told me that she wanted to quit right after she had a second child and was struggling to keep it together with less sleep than she could have ever imagined. "I was trying to make it in the TV business and I wanted to have a family and balance it all," she says. Mika was working 9 P.M. to 5 A.M. She would get home from working all night and then spend the day with her newborn and two-year-old. One Friday morning, after a long workweek, she arrived home and prepared to relieve the nanny, who had been there all night. She went up to the third floor and took her baby, who was four months old, from the babysitter. While she was trying to pay her, she walked right off the top of the huge staircase — and landed on top of her infant daughter.

She rushed her to the hospital, concerned that she had broken something in her back or injured her spinal cord. "At that point I remember thinking that work was the enemy. It was work that might have caused me to maim my child.

"I broke down to my husband and told him that I just am never going back to work," says Mika. "'I tried to be supermom, super everything, and I have fucked our lives.'"

"'Listen to me, you didn't mess up, we messed up,'" he said. "'We didn't get you enough help, and you are going back to work, you are going to get your act together, and in six months, if you want you can leave, but you have to go back.'"

She did return to work, but with a different attitude of acceptance. "I spent less time with my kids, slept more, and did only what I can do," she says. "And you know what? My kids are better for it."

If the job is fundamentally one you enjoy, think twice before walking away. Ty Stiklorius told me that after she had just given birth to her second child, she felt that there was no way she could go back to work. But her mentor, Judy McGrath, the former CEO of MTV Networks, pulled her aside one night and said, "You know, all of our daughters are gonna work one day . . . and so go home and show them a positive example of a working mom."

Only you can determine whether you should stick it out and push further or quit now and put your energies into something new. But once you've evaluated your situation, and you determine that you are in the wrong line, it's time to do something about it. As I discovered, even when you're on the fast track, it's hard to feel excited and motivated if you're speeding toward the front of the line for a job you don't really want. You will be happier and you'll go farther doing work you love.

Quitting my job at Fortress to run for public office was one of the best decisions I ever made. Yes, I lost the race. But the risk I took opened up a new world of opportunity. More important, it put me in the right line — the one I had always wanted to be on.

JUMP THE LINE

Visualize Your Bliss

Figure out what you *do* want to do. Ask yourself: What do I want to spend eight to twelve hours a day doing? What do I want to spend 30 to 40 percent of my life doing? It sounds silly, but our desire for the general cloak of success can obscure how our own personal success ought to look. It's easy to get distracted by the view from the corner office or the sound of a fancy title. It makes us forget that it is actually our day-to-day work and the impact we make that will determine whether we enjoy our job — and our life.

Similarly, it's easy to get hung up on our weaknesses instead of focusing on our strengths. What are you really good at? Given the chance, where would you excel? Betsy Morgan, president of the website TheBlaze and former head of the Huffington Post, talks about how she spent the summer before she entered business school just thinking about what she wanted to do. She researched different industries and tried to figure out what she found most interesting. She also spent a lot of time assessing what she was good at and where there was room for improvement. She asked herself what she did and did not want to get out of business school. "There's so much pressure in society to fit into certain boxes that many women don't feel confident enough to honestly assess themselves; they're too busy trying to live up to other people's expectations," says Betsy. "If you know what your strengths are ... what your weaknesses are, where you're going to need help and to not be afraid of asking for help, that is a huge advantage to any young woman starting out today."

What Betsy says is important. Be honest with yourself. Identify what you want to get out of that degree or that job. Figure out what you're passionate about.

Check Out Your Professional Worth, Go on a Date

Part of getting comfortable with quitting is knowing that you have other options and are wanted elsewhere. As Richelle Parham, the CMO of eBay, taught me, it's important to check out your "professional worth" every couple of years. What do I mean by that? Get out there and do some interviews. Do some research on job sites, including LinkedIn. Have a cup of coffee with someone you think has a cool job. Discover how people value you and what new and different opportunities might exist for you. Whatever comes of it, you will feel more empowered and better informed by knowing what your market value is. So the next time a headhunter calls you, take the call even if you are content at work! The best time to make a change is often when you don't need a new job.

Do a Self Cost-Benefit Analysis

Take out a piece of paper. Write down what you earn in one column, as well as the other material and nonmaterial benefits you get from your job (e.g., access to interesting people, a great job title, etc.). In the next column write down the amount you spend on your mental, emotional, and physical well-being because you hate your job. Yes, include the life coach, the therapist, and the dresses you buy on Gilt Groupe at noon every day because you are bored at work. Include the fights you pick with your partner, the weight you have gained or lost, and the medical bills you have incurred by your unhappiness. If the costs outweigh the benefits, you know that it is time to leave. If you are not getting a return on the investments you are making from staying at your current job, it is time to go. If you are spending more on "making you happy" to cover up how miserable you are, it's time to plan your exit strategy.

As part of this analysis, go ahead and visualize the worst that could happen if you just walked away from your job. What would be the cost of quitting tomorrow? You may be surprised at how small that number is compared to how much you spend trying to be happy. This is exactly what I did when I was contemplating quitting my job to run for office. And the truth was that the worst that could happen — losing — wasn't worse than being miserable in my job.

If You Are Thinking About Quitting, Get Prepared

No matter how much time you've spent in the wrong line, it's never too late to make a career change. I have met women who didn't discover their calling until they were well into their fifties. If you do decide that it's time to take the plunge, make sure you are prepared. You'll need to start saving money now, as there will be a financial cost to leaving your job, especially if you don't have another one lined up. You'll also have to prepare yourself emotionally. Not having a job is hard, especially if it takes time to find a new one you love. During this period you will question your worth and maybe even feel like a loser — trust me, I did! But you're not: You're a brave woman who is ready to follow her dreams.

Finally, remember to leave your organization on good terms.

The world is small and you never know whom you will work with again. Give your employer plenty of notice and help find a replacement. Regardless of how you feel when you leave, continue the relationship. Join the alumni network and stay in touch with colleagues you like (and sometimes even the ones you didn't).

5

Be Authentic

IN LATE SPRING 2010, several months before the election, I was asked to do an interview with the *New York Observer*. My weekday schedule was packed with house parties thrown by voters and supporters, parades, and policy briefings, so I agreed to meet the reporter on a Sunday afternoon at a local café in the East Village. It was a blazing hot day, so I threw on a summer dress. I didn't give a tremendous amount of thought to my wardrobe selection. I was running for Congress, not running down the runway, after all.

When I tore open the paper the following day, I was horrified. "She was dressed for the oppressive heat. Black-and-white flip-flops, a sleeveless dress, D&G sunglasses perched atop long brown hair," the article observed.[1]

How was it that my flip-flops and fancy sunglasses made the piece, but my ideas about entrepreneurship and innovation were barely mentioned?

The phone started ringing nonstop. Two of my female consultants immediately offered advice. They were concerned about the impact of "D&G-gate" and recommended that I tone it down so as to not distract from my "substance."

They reminded me to wear the uniform another congress-woman had detailed: a plain black or blue suit, a long-sleeved cotton blouse, and a conservative pair of glasses, with hair in a ponytail. For the most part I listened, but I didn't follow the protocol on practical shoes. And soon enough I paid the price.

By the last days of August, the end of my campaign was in sight. I had another Sunday morning meeting with a reporter, this time Susan Dominus from the *New York Times*. The top-ics of conversation: innovation, job creation, public-private partnerships, and the DREAM Act, a bill that would create a pathway to citizenship for students, known as "DREAM-ers," who attend college or serve in the U.S. military for at least two years. We were going to spend the day in Queens meeting with supporters ranging from young folks in Astoria to Bangladeshi taxicab drivers to constituents in Dutch Kills, Queens.

Following the first newspaper debacle, I dressed exactly how society expected me to dress for most of the summer — con-servatively, with no suggestion of any sexuality. I was excited about the interview that day and wanted to look like myself, so I pulled on a dress that was bright red but conservative enough to pass the political fashion police. I slipped on my favorite shoes, a pair of Kate Spade Halle wedges. The shoes were an unusual indulgence for me, as my shoe rack comprises Aldo and Nine West, not Chanel or Christian Louboutin. But after ACL sur-gery and intense campaigning that had my knee looking like a beach ball, my doctor convinced me to invest in them. He was right: I loved their comfort.

But even my Halles couldn't get me through a full day of campaigning. After an afternoon spent on my feet and a two-hour interview on policy, I was ready for a break. As I pulled a pair of Aerosoles flip-flops from my bag, Susan looked down and asked how I had made it all day in three-inch heels.

"They're the Kate Spade wedges," I said. "They're these politician-woman shoes."

The following day, the office was buzzing with excitement over the upcoming *Times* story. The election was just weeks away. This profile could be a game changer. It was the *New York Times*!

Then Susan called. "What size shoe do you wear?" she asked.

My campaign manager's face turned bright red, and I knew we had a problem. The article came out and it was an eight-hundred-word story about my shoes.

I was speechless. This was a campaign, not a catwalk! Shouldn't my ideas come ahead of my image? How on earth was it possible that my footwear had trumped the serious issues that Susan and I had discussed over the hours we'd spent together?

Even Susan herself seemed to hint that she might be focusing on the wrong details. "I know," she wrote. "We, the news media, are not supposed to ask female candidates about their hairstyle or their choice of pantsuits over skirts or their shoes. It is irrelevant. It is trivializing. It is sexist."[2]

Yet "there was something distinctly next-generation" about my appearance. And, in her words:

But the Kate Spade wedge heels are not just one candidate's shoes. They seem to be the shoes of a circle of younger women aspiring to power or already in it, women directly and indirectly passing on to one another ways of navigating the particular challenges of being a woman in the public eye. A woman must look put-together, but not as if she is a slave to fashion; she must look groomed, but never be spotted grooming.

The "particular challenges" Susan alluded to are very real — as is the fact that I have learned from and shared tips with other women forging their paths in what is still, in many ways, a man's world. As I reflect back, I realize that as far as appearance goes, during my campaign I was waking up in the morning and going into defense mode. Having been told over and over by men and women alike that I shouldn't draw any attention to the way I look, I was altering what I wore because I wanted to be taken seriously.

And that was wrong. It was backward. It was defaulting to an old model outlined in Betty Harragan's 1977 book, *Games Mother Never Taught You,* which basically advised women to dress like men. Harragan writes that "there is, as yet, no clear-cut solution to the problem ambitious women must face in inventing a suitable costume for their business role ... the most important consideration for women is the underlying symbolism of clothing ... If your clothes don't convey the message that you are competent, able, ambitious, self-confident, reliable and authoritative, nothing you say or do will overcome the negative signals emanating from your apparel."[3]

I disagree. We should be in a different place than we were almost forty years ago. If we can take ownership over our careers, we can take ownership over our own style, and all women need not subscribe to a uniform to be taken seriously. Women should be able to wear a skirt and be treated like someone with the same size brain as a guy in pants.

Donning the "uniform" does not reflect the values of the next generation of leaders. It simply maintains the status quo. In the end, I realized I had to be myself, my whole self — secure in the knowledge that expressing my feminine side with fabulous shoes doesn't make me any less capable or powerful.

Dress the Woman, Not the Politician

There is a long tradition of women being told that they have to dress a certain way to be taken seriously. As Jessica Valenti, a feminist author and blogger, points out, when women first started wearing pants ("bloomers," they called them) the media called the outfits "ridiculous and indecent," deriding the suffragists as "vulgar women whose inordinate love of notoriety is apt to display itself in ways that induce their exclusion from respectable society."[4] Women's professional "fashions" have changed over the years: from boxy suits to mega–shoulder pads to Hillary's pantsuits to Sarah Palin's designer suits, from floppy bows on blouses to crisp white button-downs to knee-length pencil skirts. While we have had some breakthroughs like the DVF wrap dress, which, though formfitting, is accepted in the office, for the most part women are still pushed to subscribe to the uniform, the plain black men's suit and the starched white button-down shirt, and on occasion are told that if we don't, whatever repercussions may result are our fault.

A 1970 memo from NASA to its staff said, "Bear in mind that if someone forgets to treat you like a lady, it was you that elected to wear the pants."[5] Until 1993, there was a ban on women wearing pantsuits in the U.S. Senate.[6] By telling us how we can and cannot dress, society is trying to exercise its control over women.

This has continued into today. Roger McKenzie, a fashion expert on dressing for interviews on several career advice blogs, advises young women to dress like this when they are going to an interview:

- If a woman chooses to wear a skirt, the length should be at her knee, and slacks are welcome also . . .

- It is acceptable to wear short sleeves but it should be paired with a jacket or cardigan. A twin set is a good way to put this look together.
- Women also need to be aware of the way their top fits; of course cleavage is a big no no.
- When it comes to accessories, it should be kept at a minimum: nothing too flashy, heel height should not exceed 3 inches, and makeup should be very clean and natural.[7]

Let's be honest: The point of the advice above is to ensure that women don't draw attention to their sexuality. We are told to be modest, to control our clothing so that men can control themselves. We are essentially told, indirectly and directly, that we should shape our identities and make our choices based on the impact we will have on men. This is wrong. It's time for us to start making our choices based on what feels right for *us*. We must take ownership over our own bodies, and that includes recognizing that women are adults, not little girls. We can make our own decisions about how we should and should not dress.

"It's very important for women in a professional setting to find their own style — style of voice, style of dress, style of communication, style of work habits — and know what that style is," says Betsy Morgan, former CEO of the Huffington Post. "It's really hard to be a chameleon and to try to fit into someone else's style, somebody else's workplace. You stand out and you excel if you know who you are, if you have that self-identity."

Clara Shih, an entrepreneur and the youngest member of Starbucks' board of directors, also offers insight on the issue. She observes, "Earlier in my career and during the time I was in school, I sought to be 'just like the boys.' But over time, I have realized this just isn't me. I've gotten more comfortable with being different from the boys, but just as good at my job. I have consciously softened my communication style, begun sharing more of my personal side with colleagues, and stopped wearing those God-awful boxy man suits that are not flattering on most women." Women like the CEO of Yahoo!, Marissa Mayer, are breaking this fashion taboo and embracing their sense of style.[8]

Leadership is not about conformity. Dressing according to someone else's image is not empowering; it's stifling.

Being your authentic self may mean showing your arms, wearing high heels, and (gasp!) showing some leg if you want to. Props to First Lady Michelle Obama for putting a crack in the ceiling by showing her arms. When the First Lady first started baring her arms, she received criticism that her dressing was too informal and inappropriate.[9] Last time I checked, I didn't notice that it impacted her ability to do her job. Indeed, the First Lady's influence is extending into popular culture as well. In the spring of 2012, the HBO comedy series *Veep* premiered with Julia Louis-Dreyfus playing the country's first female vice president, Selina Meyer. Ernesto Martinez, the lead costume designer, described in the *New York Times* the challenge of finding outfits that would play up the character's attractiveness without undermining her authority. His muse? Michelle Obama, whom he called "the best thing that Washington, D.C., has seen in a long time."[10]

Or what about when, more recently, Hillary Clinton appeared on the cover of the Drudge Report "au naturale."[11] The headline story focused not on the secretary of state's news conference in Bangladesh but on her bare face and glasses. The Drudge Report serves as one more example of how often in the media appearance trumps substance for women. Yet rather than turn it into a drawn-out scandal surrounding Hillary's lack of makeup, a number of journalists responded with refreshing remarks about Hillary's authenticity. Suzi Parker of the *Washing-*

ton Post commented, "Hillary showed by going natural that she is more concerned about doing her job than with her image. She has always been more policy wonk than fashion diva."[12]

During a CNN interview with Jill Dougherty, Hillary responded herself. "I feel so relieved to be at the stage I'm at in my life right now, Jill, because if I want to wear my glasses, I'm wearing my glasses . . . At some point it's just not something that deserves a whole lot of time and attention. If others want to worry about it, I'll let them do the worrying for a change."[13] Republican women like Sarah Palin are bucking the trend too, with her red peep-toe pumps and stylish eyeglasses.

Lead the Way You Live

Just as we strive for authenticity in how we look, we should strive for authenticity in how we lead. That means being comfortable with the different dimensions of our own personality — in the workplace and in our personal lives. Leadership in today's ever-changing world requires a range of skills and personality.

Indra Nooyi, the CEO of PepsiCo, is a great role model for this kind of leadership. A *New York Times* article said this about her varied background and diverse interests:

> She is the chairwoman of PepsiCo, an American citizen born in India who has spoken of entering American politics one day. She was in an all-woman rock band in college. As a Yale student, she says, she wore a sari to an interview with a consulting firm and, upon getting the job, kept wearing it. She is a New York Yankees fan. She walks barefoot in the office at times, in an echo of the Indian aversion to closed shoes. She speaks in a faintly Indian accent while tossing out Americanisms like "cut my teeth."[14]

Indra is unabashed in putting forward all of her dimensions to create a unique leadership style. From embracing her ethnicity by wearing saris to meetings to openly talking about the challenges she faces in balancing work and family as the mother of two girls, Indra offers all sides of herself to her role as CEO.[15] And as a CEO who is also a woman of color, this has led her to focus on the issue of diversity — but it's not just talk. In fact, she ties 50 percent of her bonus to her "people goals," one of which is increasing diversity.[16]

The future of leadership — for women and men alike — will be characterized by a management style that reflects a leader's personal style. The late founder of Apple, Steve Jobs, loved rocking his black turtlenecks, cried openly, and was unapologetic about his dictatorial management style. As a leader, he embraced every quirky side of himself, and many argue that these very quirks were what made Jobs so successful and creative.

Early models of leadership taught women that in order to succeed you had to behave like a man; later ones told us to find that perfect blend of both masculine and feminine traits.[17] Feminine attributes include being collaborative, relationship driven, and team oriented. Masculine traits include embracing risk, learning how to manage up, and asking for what you want. According to Mika Brzezinski's book *Knowing Your Value: Women, Money, and Getting What You're Worth,* we were taught to be aggressive and assertive, and to use foul language, but balance that with collaboration and kindness.[18] I'm confused. Are you too?

The problem is that for many of the women I have interviewed, neither leadership style feels natural. Simply copying what the boys are doing actually hurts us, because as I described in Chapter 3, women are not rewarded in the workplace for embodying what is seen as stereotypically male behavior.

Blending both masculine and feminine traits makes some sense, but it still takes away from our own authenticity and feels passé, because it assumes that our gender is the sole determiner of what attributes we have. As a woman, I am comfortable being assertive. When I am assertive, it doesn't mean that I am acting like a man; it means I am being myself.

It is true that by nature women are probably better multi-taskers because we traditionally have had to juggle more roles.[19] As Tina Sharkey, the global president and chairman for Baby-Center, said at eBay's Women's Initiative Network leadership conference, "Women are the fixers. Part of our gender is that we are constantly called in to do the work." This is also what makes women so valuable. I have heard time and time again from female and male bosses that mothers are often the most productive workers. They are more efficient with their time and they want to do well because they know they are role models for their children. "My daughter made me more ambitious and much more able to push myself, because I was pushing myself for her," says Valerie Jarrett, senior adviser to President Obama.[20] So when a mother comes in your door, whether you are her colleague or her employer, see her as an asset and not a liability.

If we want to successfully change work culture, we have to be the women on the front lines paving the way and defining the new norms for desirable leadership traits. Some of those new norms may be leading from the heart, building a sense of community, doing what is right and not what is easy. If we succeed in that endeavor, we will not only redefine what it means to be a leader, but we will also ascend in the leadership ranks.

A recent study by the *Harvard Business Review* shows that women are breaking ground when it comes to leadership within organizations and corporations. While the study finds that the majority of leaders are still men, it reveals that a majority of female leaders are perceived to be better leaders than their male counterparts.[21] Women are perceived to be much more effective executives and top managers by a margin of about 10 percent.[22] The *Harvard Business Review* presents encouraging information about the perception of female leadership. Now it is time for more women to take office, run companies, and start small businesses so that our generation can lead the way fearlessly.

Of course, that doesn't mean I am unaware of the unconscious bias that still plays out in the workplace. There is a social and professional risk to being a powerful woman. But the more female role models we have who don't hide who they are or conform to conventional norms, the faster we will be able to change these stereotypes. Additionally, this will also mean that we will create a work culture where performance is the most important thing and if you work hard, you will be rewarded.

Make Time for Life

To be authentic leaders, we must also pay attention to our personal needs. For too long, women have been telling themselves how they "should" behave or the things they "have" to do in order to be seen as successful. We have been striving to conform to an ideal that is not who we are, but only who we think we should be. This can spur us to make decisions to please others, instead of ourselves.

Embracing our multidimensional selves means acknowledging the importance of having a personal life. I have a lot of girlfriends who are in their mid-thirties and are having personal meltdowns. They are burned out at work and realize that they have been pushing so hard professionally that they have not taken inventory of their personal lives and needs. Part of embracing our authentic self means being honest about what we are looking for in life, and that can include finding a partner.

When I was first searching for my partner, I wanted to find my male alpha equivalent. It didn't go very well; it was also not the right path to helping me find my authentic self. The hard truth is that often an alpha man or woman is not going to be okay putting his or her career on hold for yours. What I learned is that the most important thing is to find a partner who is going to make your dreams his or her dreams. Increasingly, young women are beginning to understand this and prioritize a healthy, supportive relationship as one of their key measures of what makes them successful and fulfilled. In fact, a recent study by Pew found that the percentage of women between the ages of eighteen and thirty-four who said that a successful marriage is one of the most important things they value in their lives has risen 9 percentage points since 1997, from 28 percent to 37 percent.[23]

I got over the alpha male search and came up with a new plan: My mantra was to spend my life with my best friend. The person you choose will be the most important decision you make, so you must not take it lightly. Be honest about where you want to go and the role you need your partner to play in helping you get there. No one needs to be keeping score. You have to find someone who also wants to change gender norms with you. Many women whom I interviewed were forthright about the fact that they are ambitious and are comfortable with it because of the role their fathers or partners have played in their lives. I cannot stress enough how important it is to find the right person to support you and your ambitions, because we will not get parity in the workplace until we get parity at home. In the United States, married women do about 70 to 80 percent of the housework.[24] When a woman gets married, the number of hours she spends doing housework increases, whereas for men it stays about the same. When a couple has a child, the mother's housework increases three times more than the father's.

Parity at home is essential. One of the most fascinating facts about Gloria Steinem was that as a little girl her father was her primary caretaker because her mother was battling a mental illness.[25] Because of this, Gloria was free from this notion and the accompanying guilt that mothers should be the primary caretaker, which many of the other women in her generation felt. When Tiffany Dufu spoke to an audience at PricewaterhouseCoopers, someone asked her about this "guilt." A woman said, "You seem like you have no guilt whatsoever about your relationship with your kids." Tiffany has two young children, and her husband, Kojo, spends almost half the year doing business in Ghana. Tiffany replied:

> Look, every woman has a list of the things that she believes are her job, are her responsibility, what she should do as a wife and mother. And they come from all over the place: They're informed by our culture, by our family, by our communities. There's a direct correlation between the amount of guilt that you have and the amount of things that can be checked off of the list you have created in your head about what you should do as a wife and mother. Really, there are only two things on my list I have to, absolutely should do as a mother. There are things I *want* to do, and does that mean that *they* don't have expectations about the things that I should do because I'm their mother? They really like scones on Saturday mornings, and they really believe that's my job, so we negotiate the scones on Saturday morning. Most women have a very long list of things that they really truly believe is their role and their responsibility and they can't meet it.

For a woman, being your authentic self also means acknowledging whether you want to have a family or not. I have talked to countless women who said they agonized over whether to put pictures of their children on their desks, fearing the photos would signal they were risky employees. I've also talked to women who chose not to have children because they were told they could not have a child and a big career. Again, we have to ask ourselves: Who has created these norms? And why must we live by them?

Interestingly, social media is forcing changes in workplace culture, as mothers and fathers can no longer pretend they are living two separate lives, one at the office and one at home. The rapid change social media has fueled has given many of us access into one another's multidimensional lives. Social media now prevents parents from sneaking out of the office to attend their daughter's first day of school, because when they post her picture on Facebook, everyone instantly knows their whereabouts. No more hiding. Transparency is liberating.

Modern leaders, male or female, should be able to acknowledge the role their families play in their professional lives. A recent study by Pew found that today nearly six in ten women (59 percent) ages eighteen to thirty-four say being a good parent is one of the most important things in their life. The share of young men who feel this way is 47 percent now, up from 39 percent in 1997.[26]

Barack Obama is the first president of the United States who demands that five days a week he is at home to have dinner with his children.[27] The First Lady and the president rarely campaign together because they always want one of them to be home with their daughters.

Many of the working mothers I spoke to said that what they are most passionate about is creating a work space where younger moms don't feel guilty about going back to work. Anne-Marie Slaughter, the former dean of the Woodrow Wilson School of

Public and International Affairs at Princeton, says, "As dean, I would outright tell people that I am going home to our children. I would consciously break down the thing about never admitting that I have a child. At the State Department I made sure the women who worked for me had more flexibility and could stay at home part of the time."

These women are comfortable leaving work at a reasonable time to pick up their kids, and it is important to them to lead by example. Katie Stanton, head of international strategy at Twitter, often brings her children on business trips. "I am very open with my colleagues about traveling with my kids — and I tweet about it," she says.

And if you are a woman at an earlier stage of your career, having a child may turn out to be what gives you the strength to ask for what you want on the job. I spoke to a TV news reporter who told me that she was renegotiating her contract when she was eight months pregnant. As a part of a dual-income family, she felt empowered when she went to the negotiating table because it wasn't about her anymore. She knew that she had to get the most she could to make sure her child had all the opportunities she could give him. Marissa Mayer was appointed CEO of Yahoo! while she was pregnant, and the company made changes, including where it would hold board meetings, to accommodate her needs.

Marissa's hire itself is a sign that times are changing, and to Yahoo!'s credit, the company hired her for her strengths and didn't see the upcoming maternity leave as a deterrent. In the United States, our workplaces must accept the reality that three-fourths of our workforce have children. We are going to have to make room for doctors' appointments, birthdays, and holiday recitals. Mothers and fathers should not have to hide the fact that part of their fulfillment in life comes from the relationships they have with their children. Once we accept this reality, we will create more accommodating workplaces.

Being your authentic self when you are a mom also means accepting that there is no such thing as balance — and that is okay. It's also okay to enjoy work, even working hard and making sacrifices, understanding that it is not "selfish."

"I fear that my generation failed to teach our daughters how fabulous it is to work, to have a demanding career. They saw us at the end of the day, when we were a little spent. And because we felt guilty about leaving them, and loving our work, we didn't talk about the satisfaction that comes from nailing a launch or closing a deal or working with a team," says Gilt Groupe's Susan Lyne. "We told them how hard it was. I think the message that they got was that you cannot have it all — and as a result, too many college-educated women are opting out of their careers when they start having kids. So we have do to better as a culture. I'm not saying there aren't tradeoffs. There are. The truth is that you can't have it all at any given moment. You always feel like one is suffering — work or your kids. But if you look back across the breadth of life and a career, you CAN have it all — and it's so worth it."

My mother was the same way. Every evening she would come home and talk about how much she hated her job and how she wished she could stay home with us. Then, after we went off to college, she retired. Her retirement lasted approximately one week. She loved being an engineer. However, she just couldn't be honest with us about it because she felt guilty leaving us.

The women of the current generation are having children much later in their lives. Only 33 percent of eighteen- to thirty-four-year-old women are married today—as compared to 73 percent of women this age in 1960.[28] And an April 2012 National Health Statistics Report found that 36 percent of college-educated women report having their first child at age thirty or above.[29] A senior vice president at an investment bank told me that she often advises women who are planning on having children to switch to a new job when they come back from maternity leave. She believes it's going to be stressful no matter what, so you might as well be looking for ways to keep growing professionally.

For many of us who are having children later in life, we don't have the option of opting out and getting back in. Instead, we have to pursue a path to parenthood and maintain our careers simultaneously. Therefore, we have to figure out how to have it all and be okay with feeling like we are failing either our family or our career at different points. To be "okay" with that, we must change the definition of success—and stop beating ourselves up for allegedly "failing"!

Be authentic in how you look, how you lead, and how you live your life. As the late poet May Sarton said, "We have to dare to be ourselves, however frightening or strange that self may prove to be."[30]

JUMP THE LINE

Wear What You Want!

As crazy as this might sound, we will know we have made it when we can wear what we want and still be taken seriously. The takeaway: Wear what you want to exercise your power and sexuality. There's no reason not to. Even when you try to conform to cultural norms, critics will still likely find something to lambaste you about anyway. If a boss or a coworker makes a derogatory comment about what you are wearing, tell them where to go. Just be yourself.

Celebrate Your Other Dimensions

Randi Zuckerberg is not only a skilled technology executive, but she's also a fabulous singer. She once told me an incredible story on how her multidimensionality was perceived by colleagues:

> A couple of years ago I was asked to represent Facebook at Davos. At the end of the night they have all these world leaders do karaoke. You can see Obama doing karaoke with Sarkozy. I am there taking it all in, and then I decide to go for it and sing. The next day, the *Financial Times* writes about my singing and says how good I was. Some of my friends and mentors lose it. They say it was unprofessional of me to sing: that I denigrated my intellectual achievements, that I have to be either serious or fun, but I cannot be both. If Mark had sung, they would have praised him and said that it shows how he can be human. But it was different that I did because I was a woman.

Although she was chastised, Randi says she has no regrets about showcasing her musical talent. "I want to show the world that you can be a well-rounded businesswoman and be fun and silly and feminine," she explains. "That you can be an incredible singer and be a successful businesswoman and you don't have to hide who you are in fear of not being taken seriously."

Randi is right. The more open women are about the richness and multidimensional aspects of their lives, the more acceptable it will become to simply act like ourselves — and the more effective we will be as leaders.

So if you have children, put their pictures on your desk. Talk about your children; announce loudly that you are leaving at 5:30 to take your kids to a soccer game. It is up to us to change the culture. Encourage your partner to do the same. This battle to show that being a parent is part of who you are as a person will not be won by women alone. Fathers need to stand by our sides and acknowledge the role that family plays in who we are.

Similarly, be comfortable showcasing the other sides of yourself, whether it's wearing a sari to an interview or showing off your musical talent. Proudly display all of your dimensions.

Identify Your Style of Leadership

Find inspiration from other strong women who are comfortable being feminine and powerful at the same time. Visit makers.com, where you will find more than a thousand videos of the stories of extraordinary women who have brought about change in a variety of industries and professions. Understand what differentiates them and then find what differentiates you. Find your own voice. Be you and don't change your behavior to conform to what you think a leader looks or sounds like.

At one of my interview sessions, a young woman said that we all must acknowledge that we have self-doubt. At the same time, we must manage other people's perceptions of ourselves and be comfortable projecting a competent and confident persona. Eventually, it becomes a self-fulfilling prophecy. It may be that critics will judge you no matter what, but if you are confident, their opinions won't matter as much because you won't have given them the power to cause you to doubt.

Make Peace with Yourself

Many moms tell me they feel like they have to be martyrs. The so-called Mommy Wars, which pit stay-at-home moms against working mothers, don't help. We have to stop judging one another and ourselves for the choices we make in our lives.

We have to learn that we can't *do* it all in order to have it all.

Sometimes not doing it all means knowing when to delegate and building a great "home team" of people who can help. No one can do it all, and no one should feel guilty about that. "I realized that it's okay to have a nanny or lean on my own mom. My responsibility is to make sure my son feels loved twenty-four/seven, but it doesn't have to be by me," Randi Zuckerberg told me. "I am much better when I can be with him on my terms instead of his terms. I want him to see his mom contributing to society and being a leader. I want him to grow up in a world where women are leaders." Who doesn't want that? By raising our children in a way that shows them women have important and fulfilling roles in all aspects of their lives, we can make it the new normal — and all achieve better, more productive, and more meaningful lives.

6

Building a Sisterhood for the Twenty-first Century

IN OCTOBER OF 2011, I was speaking at a panel for Running Start, an organization that inspires young women to run for office. The auditorium was full of confident and eager female high school students, my favorite kind. Afterward, as I was getting ready to leave, a young woman boldly approached me and proclaimed, "Hi, my name is Paige Wallace. I am going to be president of the United States one day, and no one from my high school has ever gone to an Ivy League school. I want to be the first. I want to go to Harvard. Can you help me?" Loving her audacious ambition, I told her that of course I would help her and gave her my email address. Since I meet many young women like Paige at these panels and usually offer to help though they often don't reach out (because they are afraid to follow up and ask), I never expected to hear back from her. But two days later, I looked at my in-box, and there she was. Paige Wallace. Over the course of the year, Paige became an important figure in my life. I took her to Harvard, and together we went through the anxiety of applying to the school, the pain of not getting into our dream school, and the confusion of the financial aid process. During that time, Paige taught me about courage, perseverance, and confidence. She also taught me about the importance of sisterhood.

I would never have run for office if the women in my life did not encourage me to run. Like many of you, I owe a great deal to women who have taken an interest in my life and career, and who have guided me along the way. Over the years, I've built a sisterhood that includes women from diverse backgrounds, in different professions, at various stages in their lives. They have become the foundation of my support system. I was guided and mentored by women's organizations that helped me believe in myself. I was a member of the Women's Leadership Forum at the Democratic National Convention and spoke at the annual WLF breakfast. I served on the board of the Women's Campaign School at Yale University.

I was also fortunate to be part of a tight group of women in New York who were Hillary Clinton's closest supporters. These women were my friends and my political mothers. I first met Hillary in 1996 when I worked on the Clinton-Gore campaign. We reconnected eight years later when I was working on John Kerry's campaign and had the opportunity to introduce her at a political event for Kerry. After that, she took an interest in my life, asked me to introduce her at events, and encouraged me to be politically active.

When I decided to run for Congress, my political mothers were my home team — they believed in me and they were always there to push me to do my best.

I experienced the true power of the sisterhood during my campaign. Many wise women supported me by providing financial donations so I could build my campaign operation. Several women in the media supported me by pulling on their editors' sleeves and saying to them, "You have to check out this woman."

There were so many women who used their positions of power to reach back and make sure the media paid attention to me and covered my race. They were the ones who helped build a movement for me — and I believe this kind of movement can be replicated by any woman to help her achieve her goals.

Lifting Each Other Up

My experience is not unique. The history of American women is one rooted in sisterhood. Our mothers and grandmothers banded together to not only support one another on an individual level, but also to advance women's rights more broadly. Thanks to the progress they enabled in terms of our reproductive rights and access to educational opportunities, women now participate in every sector of public life and are gaining power and influence in those sectors.

Today, 36 percent of women ages twenty-five to twenty-nine hold a bachelor's degree, compared to 28 percent of men.[1] Nearly half of the workforce is female, and women are the majority of workers in nine out of the ten highest-growth industries.[2] We've also advanced in leadership positions. Right now, more than 20 million women have influence over hiring decisions.[3] Middle management is now more than 34 percent female, while senior leadership is 21 percent female.[4] Women also have tremendous purchasing power. We control nearly 60 percent of the wealth in the United States and we make almost 85 percent of all purchases.[5] We are spending almost $5 trillion annually — an astounding half of U.S. GDP.

But today's women also have the benefit of technology that connects us in ways that our grandmothers only dreamed of. And women dominate key segments of the digital space. Facebook, Zynga, Groupon, and Twitter — often referred to as the "Four Horsemen" of the consumer web — have a majority of female users. We are also active digital citizens. On Facebook, 62 percent of all messages, updates, and comments can be attributed to women.[6] Women tweet more, follow more people, and on average have more followers than men.

As a result of our increased power in the workplace and increased presence on the web, we have at our disposal the tools and the strength in numbers to build an even more powerful sisterhood — one that can have a profound impact on the lives of women and the direction of our nation. Sustaining the gains women have made, lifting up more low-income and minority women, and paving the way for our daughters will take all of our strength. And we have an obligation to build up this sisterhood for the twenty-first century, not just for ourselves, but for generations to come.

We have risen from the shoulders of giants. The sisterhood of the twentieth century enabled progress for women in education, the workplace, our bodies, and politics. In 1972 they fought to pass Title IX, which allowed countless young women opportunities in academics and athletics by prohibiting sex discrimination in educational facilities that received federal funding. They fought to end the ability of federally funded schools of higher education to legally discriminate on the basis of gender.[7] They fought for the passage of the Equal Pay Act of 1963, which required men and women receive equal wages for equal work.[8] They fought to end discrimination by corporations against women and pregnant women. They fought for us to have control over our bodies, legalizing contraception and abortion. They were trailblazers in politics and ran for office at the highest level, helping break down barriers for my generation.

What Does the Twenty-first-Century Sisterhood Look Like?

The sisterhood of the twenty-first century needs to be cross-generational. From various interviews, I have heard about the tensions between Boomer women and Gen X and Gen Y women. Boomer women sometimes state that younger women are entitled and they don't want to work as hard. Younger women report that Boomer women don't want to pass the baton and don't mentor them.

Having multiple generations of women at work shouldn't be a cause for rivalry, but should be seen as a real opportunity. Relationships between older and younger women can be mutually beneficial; younger women have much to gain from their older, more experienced colleagues, and older women can benefit enormously from having the fresh perspective of their younger colleagues.

Beth Comstock, the CMO of GE, shared a powerful cross-generational relationship she had with a woman who worked for her. "She was very comfortable about giving me a reality check and saying, 'You're not going to want to hear this, but here's something you need to know'; 'Here's how people see what you just did,'" says Beth. "She had great confidence and I often think, 'Wow, I'd love my daughters to be like her.'"

It's this type of relationship, built on honesty and support, that Beth values most. "As I think now of what I'm most proud of in my life, with respect to my career, it's my network; I wouldn't trade it for anything," she says. "It's men, it's women, but I'm also finding as I'm getting older that a women's network is more important than ever. I want to connect with wiser women who can sort of help navigate the way for me and I want to be inspired by younger women who are doing things that I could only have dreamed."

It's nothing new that women want these supportive cross-generational relationships. In the study "Bookend Generations: Leveraging Talent and Finding Common Ground," Sylvia Ann Hewlett and her colleagues found that 53 percent of young professional women look to Boomers for advice, while almost 60 percent of Boomers say they enjoy supporting younger women.[9]

Mentorship and Sponsorship

We all know mentorship is important. In a 2009 *USA Today* study of female CEOs, board chairs, and company founders, thirty-three of the thirty-four who responded identified a man as the one mentor who had the most influence on their careers.[10] What about women mentors? More than a majority of the women I interviewed for this book reported that they did not have a female mentor.

We need women mentors, but what we need even more are women sponsors. A sponsor is someone who helps you advance in your career by making connections on your behalf to other senior leaders or people outside of your immediate work sphere. They open up opportunities that you would not have access to otherwise. Mentors offer advice; sponsors do the legwork that actually gets you there.[11]

Sponsorship is helping to advance more women in traditionally male industries. For example, sponsorship in the start-up world has helped more female entrepreneurs get off the ground. Twenty percent of women sought start-up capital in 2011, up from 12.6 percent in 2000.[12] In Silicon Valley, Facebook COO Sheryl Sandberg hosts regular dinners, bringing together female entrepreneurs and aspiring entrepreneurs, to build a sisterhood of innovative women.

Sponsorship has also been shown to lead to increased pay for women. A 2011 study done by the Center for Talent Innovation showed that "sponsorship can result in as much as a 30 percent increase in promotions, pay raises and stretch assignments for a protégé."[13] By having someone recommend you for key assignments or provide strategic career advice, sponsors help women receive appropriate recognition for their accomplishments. Yet studies demonstrate that women are being under-sponsored compared to men.[14]

Whether we like it or not, every workforce is ruled by some level of internal politics. Back-room advocacy happens all the time, which is why we need more women in those rooms. We can't turn our backs to this reality and deem it a game we don't want to play.[15] Women need individuals who will use their own influence to advocate for seniority and better work assignments.

Hiring and Promoting Women When Possible

A stronger sisterhood can and will exert real pressure on the glass ceiling. As more women rise up into positions of power, they will have the opportunity to give back and make sure that they hire women, and that the pool of applicants for any given job has enough women.

There are several shining examples of women who have mentored and sponsored younger women in their field and groomed them to take over their jobs. For example, when Anne M. Mulcahy was CEO of Xerox, she handpicked her senior vice president, Ursula Burns, to be her successor. The *New York Times* noted that it was "the first time a female chief executive has replaced another female chief executive at a Fortune

500 company."[16] Ursula also became the first African American woman to run a *Fortune* 500 company.

Some women support their sisters by appointing them in various positions within an organization so that together they form a critical mass and can influence organizational decisions. For example, as secretary of state, Hillary Clinton vastly expanded the number of women employees at the State Department. While Hillary did not hire solely on the basis of sex, she prioritized hiring people of different backgrounds. Anne-Marie Slaughter believes the increased number of women helped develop a supportive culture that had an impact on workplace discussions:

> The women would pick up on each other's comments when we were in meetings. If one woman said something that got ignored, another woman would pick up her comment and give credit to her. Secretary Clinton also refocused the department on issues impacting women and children. These issues have historically been considered "soft" (which is a whole other problem of bias), but because of Clinton's reputation for being tough, nobody questioned her decision.

Washington runs on information and information runs through networks. In the White House, the networks are still mostly male because men are the ones in the top positions. At the State Department, because more women held high-level positions throughout the organization, the network was open to women.

Another great example of a sisterhood within an organization is the team of women that Michèle Flournoy has built at the Pentagon. One of the virtues of this approach, which Michèle's case especially illustrates, is that women can help other women gain a foothold in arenas that may have previously been considered male domains. Heather Hurlburt, executive director at the National Security Network, has applied the same approach, hiring an unusually high number of women in NSN's leadership ranks.

The great thing about the twenty-first century is that we can take advantage of new technologies to build and sustain our professional networks. Sites such as CafeMom, Sandbox, MomsRising, the Muse, iVillage, Kaboose, the Levo League, WIE, the Moxie Exchange Movement, Change the Ratio, and 85 Broads that seek to create communities and reinforce connections through shared interests and gatherings are shaping and developing a female community online. Sandbox, for example, strives to connect young leaders across the globe and "accelerate" success by creating a virtual community of support. The organization StartOut just launched a program to mentor lesbian entrepreneurs by creating programming opportunities, connecting members, and developing resources in the face of discrimination to promote a strong community.

Diversity and Inclusion

The new sisterhood also needs to have a real commitment to diversity. Oftentimes our twentieth-century sisters were criticized for not being diverse when it came to age, race, and sexual orientation. This new sisterhood must make sure that women of color are represented in government and in the corporate sector. In politics, women of color are often discouraged from running by another office holder or a political party official. Statistics show that 42 percent of women of color compared to 28 percent of nonminority women are dissuaded from running for office.[17] This is particularly troubling because African American women make up 8.1 percent and Latina women are 2.9 percent of all state legislators and we desperately need more diverse women in office.[18]

The Call to Action

Nothing will change if we, as women, don't take the first step. Ladies, it's time to heed the call to action. We need to start doing business with one another. New, emerging female networks are focused on how they can do exactly that. In Omaha, Nebraska, ChicConect's mission statement is to give:

> YOU the opportunity to "connect" face-to-face with other members and socialize, network, and attend special events. Whether you are new to the area, a long-time resident, a stay at home mom, work from home, own a business, want to own a business, go to a job everyday, or just sit home all day and watch soap operas and eat bonbons (lucky you). . . there are always opportunities out there for You![19]

Sara Haider, an engineer at Twitter, runs the Women in Engineering group at Twitter, which brings women together to talk about technical topics — not "women topics." Sara explains, "The women at Twitter are not just having a conversation about why there are not enough women in engineering; they are doing something about it by actively recruiting young women and engaging them to be passionate about science, math, engineering, and technology."

In New York, angel investor Joanne Wilson and her Women Entrepreneurs Festival and media blogger Rachel Sklar and her Change the Ratio group are similar examples. These women launched organizations that serve to introduce women to women in an effort to help get them capital and resources to start their own companies.

CHALLENGES

Owning Our Competitive Spirit

For this modern sisterhood to reach its fullest potential, we need to acknowledge, examine, and overcome attitudes that hold us back.

First, we have to do away with the "limited resource theory." During my race, there were myriad reasons why people decided not to vote for me or support my campaign, and I understood that. That's just politics. Democracy is about having choices.

There's a saying in politics: When women run, they win. I have a problem with that on a few counts. Most of all, it assumes inherently that women can't run against each other. It is true that primaries between two viable females are still relatively rare. According to the Center for American Women and Politics at Rutgers University, there were only thirteen House races between two women in 2010.[20] Part of this may be attributed to the fact that fewer women run for office overall. Still, things are changing, and the political sphere needs to make room for more women to vie against each other for office. After all, the goal isn't to simply get any woman into office. It's to give voters the choice to vote for the best woman.

That means that women will have to compete against each other — and there's nothing wrong with that. In fact, part of bringing the sisterhood into the twenty-first century is understanding that women can be simultaneously competitive and at the same time teammates. In some ways, this is one of the legacies of Title IX, the law that requires educational institutions that receive federal funding to implement gender equity in key areas, including athletics. The law was a huge boon to women's sports in schools and led to generations of little girls finding a place on the basketball court or soccer field.

I grew up in a post–Title IX world, and thanks in large part to participating in team sports, I have had the privilege of competing with and against women my whole life. When I entered the workforce, going up against other women to advance wasn't something foreign or uncomfortable. And it certainly did not need to engender negative feelings. If anything, I've been excited to see so many qualified, bright women advancing.

According to her study on Title IX and its effect on women's careers, Wharton professor and economist Betsey Stevenson found that "increased athletic opportunities for girls in high school and college account for about 4 percent of the rise in the female labor force, and about 15 percent of the rise in women employed in 'male' occupations, like construction, since 1972."[21]

Sarah Robb O'Hagan, president of Gatorade, attributes her positive attitude toward ambition and failure to competitive sports. Being an athlete increased her confidence, taught her to take risks, and encouraged her to learn from her failures. These lessons may have been learned on the athletic field, but they were carried into the classroom and the boardroom.

Many women are naturally more collaborative and perhaps feel that embracing competition is at odds with the impulse to share and be generous. But competition is a healthy part of life, and it doesn't necessarily have to lead to hostility. In fact, pushing each other to compete — whether it's for a promotion or for public office — ought to be an integral component of our twenty-first-century sisterhood.

JUMP THE LINE

Be a Mentor or a Sponsor

You don't need to be in senior management to mentor or sponsor a woman. No matter where you are in your career, you can share your knowledge and insights with another woman. I call this the hookup mentorship model, where you connect another woman — most likely a peer — to whatever resource she might need that you have access to.

Horizontal mentorship can be just as powerful as vertical relationships. While there is much to learn from women who are senior to us, there is equally as much to gain from women who are in the same peer group.

Many of us may already be at a point where we can help our peers in big ways and small. If you do not have access to a woman who is more senior than you professionally, ask your peers for help. That may mean asking them to introduce you to someone influential in their network. It may mean asking them to review your résumé, practice a salary negotiation with you, or share one of your accomplishments on Facebook. And, of course, it means that you do the same for them. These are little things you can do to hook a sister up. Open up your networks; be generous. Regardless of how tired I am or how busy, I commit to making sure I have time in my schedule for a coffee or a call or an email exchange.

A quick phone conversation can change another sister's life. I introduced my friend Dee Poku to Audrey MacLean, a powerful venture capitalist and entrepreneur in Silicon Valley. Flash backward twenty years ago: Audrey was thirty-one years old and raising money for her first business. She was one of the first female entrepreneurs in Silicon Valley. In the middle of her presentation, one of the investors, a man, asked, "Audrey, I have a question for you: Are you pregnant?"

Audrey replied coyly, "Do you know why we wanted you in this investment round? Because you are so incredibly observant."

"Oh my God, you are pregnant," he said. "This is a disclosure item; you should have told me."

Audrey looked at him, stuck out her stomach, and said, "Consider it disclosed. I have a two-year-old daughter at home, and if she is going to have a mother who has a start-up, she should have a buddy."

She then went on to tell him how this was the right time to have the baby, as the gestation time on the product was longer than the gestation period for the baby. He looked at Audrey and then looked at his assistant and said, "Wow, Audrey just convinced me and said this is in our best interest."

Dee was in a similar situation in 2012. She had recently learned she was pregnant and felt like she needed to disclose it to the main investor of her start-up company, WIE Network. I introduced Dee to Audrey, and Audrey was able to walk Dee through exactly how she should have a conversation with that investor. Because of that advice, Dee was able to secure funding for her company.

There are many ways to be a mentor or sponsor. Seek out younger women in your office and take them out to coffee to learn more about their career interests. Respond to alumni from your college or grad school who are seeking career advice. Be creative. Over the last year or so, I've thrown numerous "interview parties," which brought diverse groups of women together to have a real dialogue on how we can build a twenty-first-century model for female leadership. Many lasting support relationships grew out of those dinners. You can do the same.

Host a "women who don't wait in line" house party and invite women to come share their experiences and networks.

You can also sign up for mentorship programs like Big Sister. Mentoring at-risk girls is a fantastic way to give back to your community and expand the pipeline of badass women.

I recently founded a nonprofit called Girls Who Code, which teaches teenage girls how to code in computer languages. Each participant is paired with a mentor who is an entrepreneur or an engineer. We need to pull in more young women who may never otherwise have the opportunity to achieve, and guide them to the resources, people, and, most of all, confidence that will empower them to overcome their circumstances and do great things.

Pick a Woman

If you are one of those more than 20 million women who have power over hiring decisions, use it. Perhaps you can find your own successor; if so, try to get a woman! Do what Hillary Clinton did at the State Department. Find the most qualified candidates you can, and if you have an opportunity to break a gender barrier at your company, break it. The boys have been doing it for years. It is our time now.

Work with your human resources department to alter job descriptions so that they will attract women in equal numbers. See if they are willing to add an equal opportunity line to the description, like "Women and minorities are encouraged to apply." Find out where job descriptions for your company are being posted. Are they being circulated widely enough to reach networks of women? Or are they only being passed by word of mouth? Sometimes, especially in companies where leadership is dominated by men, job listings don't even get in front of women in the first place. Get creative and make suggestions to change that. You don't need to be the boss to make suggestions.

Have Each Other's Back

Being supportive means everything from telling each other when we have lipstick on our teeth to bigger things like keeping our eyes and ears open for opportunities for women in our networks.

Having each other's back can start with the way you introduce your girlfriend. Don't just say, "Meet Julie. She is awesome." Introduce her by saying, "Meet Julie. She graduated from the University of Michigan. She is a fantastic writer and is passionate about teaching math to high school students." Give her the type of introduction that showcases her accomplishments. By promoting her, who knows what doors might open?

We also have to protect each other from gossip and discrimination. If someone says something negative about a boss or colleague based on her gender, question him or her about it. Push them and yourself to question your assumptions and biases.

To be a real girls' girl, each of us has to undo and unlearn our own traumas that we may have felt when we were treated poorly by another woman. I don't want to be filled with resentment toward the women or organizations that treated me badly. I never want to treat any young woman how I was treated during my campaign.

In recent years, we've heard so much about the rise of bullying through social networks. You can help the young girls in your life from being teased, labeled, or bullied in school for alleged sexual behavior, and we can all encourage the younger generation to protect each other. Wouldn't it be great if we got our young women to a place where, instead of bullying each other for sexual behavior, they defended each other against gossip? Where, instead of falling into the age-old trap of demonizing female sexuality while glorifying male sexuality, girls stand up for themselves and collectively question the double standard?

Be Competitive and Raise the Bar for Your Own Personal Best

When we're not honest about our own goals and ambitions, we can be prone to passive-aggressive behavior. How many times have you been dishonest, with yourself and with others, about wanting a particular assignment at work, or even a great new job — and then stewed silently when someone else got what you wanted? If you want something, the first step is acknowledging what you want in order to get it.

Being a competitive person is not a bad thing. Be honest with yourself about how much you want to win and stop suppressing your feelings. This is important because suppression leads to jealousy. Also, it's imperative to understand that these feelings are genderless and it's okay to feel them.

Once you accept your own competitive spirit, practice setting higher goals for yourself to achieve. If you need help in creating a more positive attitude toward competition, join a competitive team. There are plenty of opportunities for women of all ages to join sports leagues or a competitive cooking class, and the Internet is a great way to find them. Check out Sportsvite, a website that allows you to connect with sports leagues or players in your area. Or maybe you want to set a goal with some friends: running a half marathon, doing a walkathon for charity and seeing who can raise the most money — anything to get you into the spirit of goal setting and goal achieving.

7

Taking It to the Streets

THE STORIES OF THE EXTRAORDINARY women in this book and elsewhere illustrate the potential for women to advance in ways our mothers only could have dreamed of. There's no denying that we live in very different times than American women of previous generations, with fewer barriers to entry and more access to opportunities.

Now that we're inspired, I want to talk about the things that we, as women, can actually do every day, big and small, to help advance the sisterhood even further. You can advocate for change and engage in activism from wherever you stand.

So what needs to be in our policy toolkit? What issues do we need the sisterhood to take to the streets?

In 2010, women became the majority of the workforce. Women represent well over 50 percent of college graduates. For every two men who get a college degree, three women will receive theirs. And yet the state of women in the workforce today is nowhere near what it should be. We make up less than 16.8 percent of Congress, 23.5 percent in state legislatures, 15 percent of top corporate jobs, and 24 percent of full-time professors. Women only hold 16.1 percent of seats on corporate boards, even though studies show that having more than three women on corporate boards increases investment returns.[1]

Why aren't we cashing in on our advances? Why aren't we crashing through that glass ceiling?

Anne-Marie Slaughter explains that some of the trouble might actually be in the term "breaking the glass ceiling." "The feminist movement thought that as more women entered the workforce the barriers would disappear on their own," she says. But it's no longer just about breaking the glass ceiling, Slaughter suggests. "Now we are at a time where we need a lot less of breaking down things and a lot more of building up. Building up day care, pregnancy leave, and policies and practices that are going to enable women to have successful careers and family life."

When I asked one of my interns, Lisa Hansman, a seventeen-year-old college student, what the glass ceiling means to her, she replied: "When a woman is successful in the workplace, especially in any typically male-dominated realm, the first turn of phrase that jumps into someone's mind is that she's shattered the glass ceiling." The imagery of that phrase says a lot about the era it was created in: It symbolizes a straight vertical movement, one achieved through powerful ambition and single-minded determination. This is admirable: a woman who sees what she wants and pursues it. But when a woman is on that straight vertical path, onward and upward to shatter the glass ceiling, she is also placing herself within an unbending, male-created channel — an unforgiving one that provides her little flexibility. Because these career paths are so inflexible, only with "shattering" force can a woman reach the top. For the women a couple of generations before me, this was certainly true. Instead, what my generation must be concerned with is creating a world in which the female capability — one that is, without question, equal to the male capability — can reach its full potential.

"Saying that we need to reform the way we think about career paths isn't a claim that women are not capable, but rather a judgment that women are capable of more than the current system allows us to achieve," says Anne-Marie. She is absolutely right, but creating workplaces that respect the family lives of both men and women is only one of many structural issues that we must address. To effect real change on the policies and practices that hold us back, we need to leverage our twenty-first-century sisterhood. Indeed, it is more than just an avenue for individual women to advance in their personal and professional lives. It is a platform from which we can advocate for systemic policy change that will not only lead to more women in leadership positions, but also will allow women to gain control over their personal and professional lives.

Leveling the Playing Field

When we think about how women can achieve their full economic potential, it begins with making sure that we have the freedom to exercise our basic economic, social, and political rights. That means everything from the right to get paid what a man gets paid for similar work to the right to marry who we love regardless of sexual orientation. It means being free from domestic violence and being free to raise our child while building our professional potential. It's the freedom to make choices about the lives we want to lead.

We must be able to reach our full economic potential. We must once and for all end the persistence of the gender wage gap in the workplace. If women are truly equal to men, they deserve to get paid the same for the same work. Economic equity means making sure that we empower female entrepreneurs and small business owners. No woman should have to choose between her job and having a family or her family's health and well-being. To empower working mothers who make up the majority of the female workforce, we need policies like paid parental leave and affordable child care to support working parents. Period. Additionally, we must make sure that our girls are being educated in the fields of the future, which include science, technology, engineering, and math (STEM). Right now our girls are being left behind in these areas, and we must put forth policies that will make sure they have a chance to be the leaders of tomorrow.

We must fight for our basic rights, which include our reproductive rights. All women, whether they live in New York or Virginia, have a right to contraception and reproductive health — a right to have control over their own bodies.

We must advocate for policies that will protect our political rights. That means ensuring that all of our sisters, regardless of sexual orientation, can marry whom they love. It means making sure that our immigrant sisters are protected from domestic violence and have access to higher education.

Pay Equity

Even though we are living in the twenty-first century, there is a massive gender gap when it comes to pay. Women are earning just 77 cents for every dollar a man does. Over a woman's life this amounts to more than $431,000. The wage gap is even more discriminatory for women of color. African American women earn only 69.5 cents for every dollar earned by a white male, and Latina women earn 60.5 cents for every dollar.[2] In my home state of New York, the median annual earnings for a woman is $42,113, while for men it's $50,388 a year.[3] We must end wage discrimination. If the gap in pay equity continues at this pace, it won't be until 2056 that we close the pay gap.[4]

Some argue that the pay gap exists because women choose professions that earn less, often work part time after having a child, or work fewer hours even if they are working full time.[5] It is true that women are concentrated in professions that often pay less. We must strive to change that. As employers and employees we must promote policies and offer incentives that encourage women to move into fields that pay more and that have traditionally been dominated by men.

There is no denying that occupational segregation plays a role in enhancing the pay gap.[6] More than 80 percent of graduates in the fields of food, education, health, and legal studies are women, whereas more than 80 percent of graduates in engineering, transportation, and technology are men.[7] Male-dominated professions pay more than female-dominated professions. For example, the average female food science technician makes $32,163 and 96 percent of students in the food science field are women. The average male aircraft technician makes $56,363 and 94.5 percent of students in this field are men. And within these fields there are huge wage differentials based on gender. A male food science technician makes $45,316 — $13,153 more than his female counterpart. A female aircraft technician makes $40,884 — $15,479 less than her male counterpart.[8]

So while we must encourage women to pursue careers in higher-paying industries, that will not close the gap by itself. We must still combat gender discrimination by speaking out against the gender pay gap that exists in many industries. Start with yourself. Take a negotiation workshop, learn your worth in the market, and practice negotiating for a higher salary.

Support for Women Entrepreneurs

Some have argued that women have turned to entrepreneurship because of the pervasive wage gap. One out of eleven women in America runs her own business. As of 2012, there were 8.3 million women-owned businesses, employing 7.7 million people and garnering $1.3 trillion in revenue a year.[9] From 1997 to 2007, the number of women-owned businesses skyrocketed and grew twice as fast as male-owned firms.[10] However, while women's businesses are growing, according to *The State of Women-Owned Businesses Report*, commissioned by American Express OPEN, women-owned businesses account for only 29 percent of all enterprises, employ only 6 percent of our national workforce, and make up only 4 percent of business revenues.[11] Only one in five women who own businesses have revenues over $1 million.[12]

This disparity between the number of women-owned businesses and the amount of revenue they generate demonstrates that women business owners need more support.

Work-Life Balance

Ninety percent of American mothers and 95 percent of American fathers report having an unbalanced work-life load. The United States has some of the most hostile work-family policies in the world; for example, we are the only industrialized nation to not offer government-mandated paid maternal leave. There are 178 countries that offer paid leave for new moms. The United States is left in the company of Swaziland and Papua New Guinea.[13]

As Cali Yost, CEO and founder of Work+Life Fit, says, "There are workplace and public policies that plan for time off and income replacement in case of illness or injury. There are 401(k)s and social security for when you retire and can no longer work. Why isn't there a coordinated, uniform workplace and public policy that offers time off and at least partial income replacement when people, inevitably, have babies or an aging parent needs care?"[14]

The Family and Medical Leave Act of 1993 (FMLA) was certainly a step in the right direction (though that step happened twenty years ago!). But the law only requires employers to provide unpaid leave to a mother or a father after having a child, which poses a huge cost to families. It also excludes small business and companies with less than fifty employees, which make up more than half of the employers of our workforce.[15] Many of the parents who are employed by small businesses are the ones least able to afford unpaid leave in the first place.

Only a handful of states, including California and New Jersey, offer six weeks of paid time for new parents.[16] Think about that. A mother has to take an unpaid "sick" day to take care of her newborn. As a nation we are signaling that having children is a sickness.

Family-friendly policies are not just for women. According to a 2011 study by the Families and Work Institute, 87 percent of all employees, including men, place workplace flexibility as the top consideration when looking for new employment.[17] Millennial fathers report spending more time with their children than previous generations. Even though more than 50 percent of married couples depend on both partners' income, women are still bearing the domestic burden.[18]

The traditional roles of parenthood don't exist for many younger generations of men, and the fact that they are taking more responsibility in the home is a welcome evolution; women will not be equal in the workplace until they are equal at home.

But the workplace needs to similarly evolve to acknowledge these new attitudes about family roles. Family-friendly policies free up men to be more equal partners at home. Policies such as flexible work arrangements that allow for job sharing or parents to work remotely or spend less time in the office can lead to greater sharing of parental obligations between partners.

Affordable Child Care

Women make up almost half the U.S. labor force, but despite this significant rise since 1970, America still lacks the infrastructure for an affordable nationwide child-care program. Since more working mothers are entering the workforce, employers and the government will have to address the issue of affordable child-care options. More than 66 percent of women with children under the age of seventeen work full or part time. However, child-care programs have not adapted to this dynamic shift.[19]

By not investing in nationwide affordable child-care programs, our society is keeping an airtight glass ceiling on women rising in the labor force.[20] We can engage companies in this cause by providing tax breaks to businesses that help their employees find child-care options and provide on-site child-care services at their workplace.

Closing the STEM Gap

While 60 percent of bachelor's degrees are obtained by women, only 20 percent of engineering, computer science, and mathematics students are female.[21] Five percent of computer science degrees are earned by minority women.[22]

In 2009, there were 2.5 million college-educated women

with STEM (science, technology, engineering, and math) degrees versus 6.7 million men. Compare this to the overall labor force, where there are 21.4 million women and 22.2 million men with bachelor's degrees.[23] The gap is huge!

This underrepresentation of women in STEM has remained constant over the past decade even though the number of women graduating with bachelor's degrees has increased. Right now women account for only 24 percent of the workforce in the growing science and technical fields.[24] One out of every seven engineers in the United States is a woman.[25]

By 2018, a majority of the job openings will be for software engineers, accountants, teachers, network/data communications analysts, and computer systems analysts, compared with any other jobs requiring a bachelor's degree.[26] In fact, a 2011 report by the Department of Commerce showed a 17 percent growth estimate for STEM jobs from 2008 to 2018, compared to 9.8 percent for non-STEM jobs in the same period.[27] STEM workers earn 26 percent more than non-STEM workers.[28] Interestingly, women in STEM are less likely to face the gender pay gap discussed above than any other profession. For example, female computer programmers make 93 cents on every dollar earned by a man, compared to 77 cents on every dollar for other professions.[29]

At a time when the public and private sectors are struggling to create jobs, the technology sector is struggling to fill innumerable open positions. While qualified software engineers, product managers, and data scientists are in demand, today's students are not adequately equipped with the knowledge and skills needed to pursue STEM careers. In fact, compared to their peers in other developed nations, U.S. students are behind in both science and math.[30] And while youth are struggling to meet the demands of today's STEM job market, it is women — particularly minority women — who are being left behind because they are not entering STEM career fields.

We have to increase the pipeline of female engineers and put forth policies that will encourage women to go the distance in science, technology, engineering, and math. This starts with our girls. We have to change gender stereotypes that exist in our society that tell young women that computer science and engineering are not for them because they are not good at it. Also we have to combat the myth that girls are not interested in math, science, engineering, or technology. From the talking Barbie that said, "Math class is tough" to Forever 21's T-shirt for girls that had the slogan ALLERGIC TO ALGEBRA, popular culture is hurting this cause.

There is a false perception that girls fare better in English and don't perform as well as boys do in math and in science. In fact, according to a study done by the National Assessment of Educational Progress, girls and boys in high school perform the same in math and science; girls actually get better grades in math and science, but boys perform better on standardized tests in these subjects.[31]

Furthermore, there's the perpetuated myth that girls are not exploring STEM degrees because they are not interested in the subject. In fact, a 2012 study by the Girl Scouts found that 74 percent of high school girls across the nation are interested in STEM fields.[32] However, a 2009 poll found that only 32 percent of thirteen- to seventeen-year-old girls compared to 74 percent of boys in the same age range thought that computing was an acceptable college major.[33]

Why do girls feel that way? It has nothing to do with aptitude or interest, but everything to do with cultural stereotypes, perceptions, and the lack of female role models.

Regardless of their own real performance, it is clear that

girls are responding to preconceived notions that boys are better at these subjects. Research suggests that the "perception of one's ability or capability is more important for a girl than her actual ability or knowledge, and changing this perception can lead to more entry into STEM domains."[34] Clara Shih, the youngest woman on Starbucks' board, talks about how she was affected by this as a young woman. "I figured out on graduation day that the guys who puff out their chest the most in class or at work and who used to intimidate me are usually the ones who have the least to brag about. On graduation day at Stanford, I learned to my surprise that I finished number one in my computer science class. All along these guys in my class had me duped into thinking I was not nearly as smart as them."

Moreover, girls pick careers that they think will make their community or the world a better place. They simply don't think that they can make a difference by being a computer scientist or an engineer. Even girls who are studying STEM or who have completed a computer science degree in college often are not opting into STEM careers. For example, two-thirds of the girls who were on the STEM track that the Girls Scout study surveyed said they wanted to be a doctor or a veterinarian instead of computer scientist or engineer.[35] In order to get them to opt into the fields of the future, we have to show them how technology pervades every aspect of our lives; connects to other disciplines like political science, medicine, and design; and can be used to create opportunities for those in need. One of my personal regrets is that I didn't major in computer science. As an aspiring political figure who wants to help people, I could have used computer science skills to build websites for immigrant entrepreneurs or a mobile app like Forage Oakland, an innovative service created by graduate student Asiya Wadud that helps

people in her neighborhood share excess fruit from their back-
yard trees.

Finally, young women may be opting out of these fields because they are dominated by men. As Audrey MacLean told me,
"We lost decades of young women in the STEM fields because
they were consciously and unconsciously taught that the computer is a boy's toy. The technology culture is dominated by vio-
lent gaming culture."

When you walk into your first computer science class in college, the majority of your peers are still men. At both Carne-
gie Mellon University and MIT, female numbers are increasing, but only 32 percent and 30 percent, respectively, of those
enrolled in CS 101 are women.[36]

This is a deterrent for many young women. Almost half of
the girls in the Girl Scouts' 2012 study said that they would be
uncomfortable being the only girl in a STEM class.[37] We have
to increase the amount of role models for young women interested in STEM careers in order to change the ratio.

That's why, in February 2012, I founded Girls Who Code.
The mission of Girls Who Code is to educate, inspire, and
equip underserved girls ages thirteen to eighteen with the skills
and resources necessary to pursue careers in science, technology, engineering, and math. The Girls Who Code program includes an eight-week summer intensive program designed to
teach high school girls basic software development skills and is
accompanied by yearlong outreach initiatives, mentorship programs, and internship opportunities to realize each participant's
potential. In 2012 we launched in New York City, but by 2013
we plan to hold programs in five to seven more cities. The summer program takes all potential barriers — lack of confidence,
few female mentors, a connection to helping people — and ad-
dresses them head-on. Each girl is paired with a female men-

tor. In 2012 we brought in speakers from all walks of life, in every industry, to show how technology can change people's lives. Finally, every day we are working on increasing the girls' confidence by focusing on not just hard skills, but on soft skills like raising your hand and asking questions.

In one summer, we provide these young women with the skills to prepare them for careers in science, technology, engineering, and math if they so choose and help develop a robust training, network, and mentorship program to support them in pursuing opportunities in the STEM fields.

Girls Who Code is a movement. In the long term, our goal is to close the STEM gap and make computer science a mandatory requirement in high school and eventually middle school. After our first summer we are taking our eight-week curriculum to cities across the country and working to adapt the program in public schools for a yearlong or semester-long course. We also have launched Girls Who Code clubs in high schools. We know that there are just so many girls we can reach through our summer program. The movement must include working with public schools across the country. Computers are like paper and pencils, and we must make sure that no child is caught in the technology divide that exists today.

With everyone seemingly wired, the digital divide seems like the punch line of a joke on *The Daily Show*, but the divide is real. In 2010, four out of every ten homes with incomes below $25,000 reported having wired Internet access at home, compared to 93 percent of households with annual incomes exceeding $100,000.[38]

Children with computer access both at home and in school are put at an advantage because they have the ability to practice what they learned at school. We have to make sure that no child is put at a disadvantage in achieving her dreams.

Women's Reproductive Health

Reproductive freedom is a fundamental right. Yet access to reproductive health services, including legal, safe, and affordable contraception and abortion, is in jeopardy — jeopardizing, in turn, a woman's right to regulate her own body and health. As women's rights have progressed in other areas, attacks on reproductive health have persisted, with new threats surfacing in Congress and state legislatures every year.

Seven states have banned nearly all abortions twenty weeks after fertilization.[39] Twenty states currently enforce bans that outlaw abortion as early as the twelfth week of pregnancy, in violation of the standards set by the landmark Supreme Court case *Roe v. Wade.*[40] These states fail to provide reasonable exceptions for serious complications or for cases of rape and incest. The bills are also loaded with criminal penalties and heavy requirements meant to scare doctors away from performing procedures they deem medically necessary.[41]

And that is just the legislation that has passed. Bills proposing far more alarming restrictions on women's reproductive health rights are still under consideration at every level.[42] A measure permitting hospitals that receive federal funding to refuse to perform an emergency abortion — even with a woman's life at stake — recently passed the House before being rejected by the Senate.[43] Several state legislatures have considered measures that would require women seeking abortions in the early stages of pregnancy to undergo an invasive transvaginal ultrasound procedure to obtain a detailed picture of the fetus.[44] These and other measures aimed at restricting access to abortion services at best patronize and at worst endanger the lives of American women.

Central to the fight to prevent unwanted pregnancies is

affordable access to contraception—a guarantee President Obama included in the Affordable Care Act.

The vast majority of women in the United States have used contraception at some point in their lives, yet as of 2006, 36 million American women lacked insurance coverage for their prescription birth control. Studies have shown that co-pays and co-insurance are deterrents for women who would otherwise use preventative services, leading to more unintended pregnancies.[45]

This is an economic issue. Increasing access to no-cost contraception allows women and families, particularly those who are low income, to effectively plan for pregnancy. Support Planned Parenthood, NARAL, and the Center for Reproductive Rights. Join their advocacy campaigns or volunteer at a clinic to make sure women's reproductive rights are protected.

Women Immigrants

Women immigrants, documented and undocumented, make up half of all immigrants in the United States.[46] As newcomers to our country, they face unique challenges in settling down, finding economic opportunities, and supporting their families and children. We need to broaden the conversation about women's rights and opportunities to include new immigrant women and their specific needs. And we need to make sure that immigrant women are included in our twenty-first-century sisterhood.

Many immigrant women who come to the United States are highly educated and have advanced degrees; however, only 13 percent of immigrant women in America work as professionals in the United States, even though 32 percent of them had professional jobs in their native country.[47] Many of these women need programs that will enhance their English proficiency.

Many business licenses and forms in New York City as well as across the country are available only in English. This is a barrier for many immigrant women because 52 percent of immigrant women speak English less than very well.[48]

Immigrant women are also affected by specific policies that target undocumented immigrants. For example, many undocumented women cannot access higher education. Each year, about sixty-five thousand undocumented immigrant children who have grown up in the United States graduate from high school.[49] But while they are eligible to apply for college, their lack of American citizenship or legal immigration status makes it impossible for them to secure college loans. Those same factors prohibit undocumented students from finding work that would help them pay their own way through college. They are ineligible for federal financial aid, and in some states, they aren't even eligible for in-state tuition rates. The economic downturn and rising college tuition have only worsened matters. One of my mentees who is undocumented came to me in the summer of 2012. She was still in the process of finishing college. Because of her status she was unable to find work to help her pay for school. Her mother had been recently diagnosed with vertigo and was struggling to keep her hours at work and care for my mentee and her brother. Food was scarce, and my mentee was desperate to make ends meet for her family. She contemplated babysitting instead of finishing her degree and working toward her goal to be an activist in her community. We cannot continue to ask these deserving young people to defer their dreams.

In 2011, when I was the deputy public advocate, I launched the DREAM Fellowship in partnership with the New York Immigration Coalition to provide DREAMers with private aid to attend the City University of New York and pursue their dream for higher education.

In 2010, the DREAM Act offered some hope for a reprieve. The act was designed to create a pathway to citizenship for students who have attended college or served in the U.S. military for at least two years. But the DREAM Act failed to pass in the U.S. Senate. In June 2012, President Obama announced an executive order that would stop the deportations of DREAMers and grant work permits to eligible students. Around eight hundred thousand students will benefit from this deferred action.

The president's courageous executive order does not substitute for the need to pass the DREAM Act. The DREAM Act makes economic sense. If immigrant children can access higher education, they will be in a better position to contribute to our economy and will be less likely to use expensive social services. They will also be in a better position to help improve the circumstances for their families.

JUMP THE LINE

Take It to the Streets

We have to get active. We don't have to wait for Election Day to vote! You can write to your local representative, author an op-ed, start a Facebook campaign, or run for office yourself. Support women's businesses, whether it is by shopping in a woman-owned business in your community or donating to a woman's business on Kickstarter or Kiva.

It's important to stay informed about what policies are being proposed by your local, state, and national officials to either restrict or protect women's reproductive rights. Pay attention to what's happening around the country too. Even if things look fine where you live, there is a sister somewhere in another community whose rights are at risk. Read blogs like Feministing,

Generation Meh, Jezebel, the Glass Hammer, and Huffington Post Women to learn about the issues affecting women across the world right now. We need to lean on our twenty-first-century sisterhood to extend our support to women everywhere. By supporting candidates in those states who are protecting our rights, we can ensure that we will go forward, not backward. Also support online communities or social media campaigns that defend women's rights in other states. What happens to a woman in Virginia or Kansas affects a woman in New York or California.

Of course, we can't just stop with reproductive rights. As I discussed in this chapter, there are a range of issues, from pay equity to paid leave to affordable child care, that we need to advocate for. In order to get the federal and state governments and corporations in your locality to change their policies for women across the country, we may need to do something bold. This starts with understanding what your local officials' positions are on these issues. Does your representative support paid leave? What has he or she done to work with corporations in your area to encourage them to change their policies?

If the policies in your community are not progressive for women, start talking to your neighbors and activists — men and women — in your community. Learn what you can do to influence change. If that doesn't work, then it may be time to take to the streets. What it may take is a city- or nationwide coordinated walkout at our places of work to really shift the paradigm. We need to do something radical to make sure our voices are heard. Unless we demand these changes, they may never come. We have to ask our male counterparts to join us in this struggle. These are the changes we need for gender parity in all industries.

Organize in Your Workplace to Demand Better Policies for Women and Yourself

Many young women ask me whether they can have children and be at the top of their game in their profession. My answer is yes. Consider Marissa Mayer's appointment as Yahoo!'s CEO just a few months before she was due to have her first child. However, not every company is so enlightened. We must work together to change policies in the workplace that make it possible to have children and careers and make it the norm to do so. We have to advocate for family-friendly policies. This starts with understanding the policies at your workplace. Does your employer offer paid leave? Is it open to having an on-site day care? What are its policies on flex time? Don't be afraid to ask these questions for yourself or for others. Things are not changing simply because women are not asking. We can't keep on pretending that we don't have work-life issues, that everything is all good. I know you might feel as if by going in and asking these questions you are making yourself vulnerable. Perhaps you think that by even asking the question you are implying that you don't want to work hard or that you are putting yourself in the "pink ghetto."

It's time to shift this line of thinking. Remember that these issues affect men and women alike, and as you ask these questions, bring your male allies with you, because they have the same needs as you. If you are asking for yourself, as Cali Yost says, meet with your boss with a plan: "Go in to that meeting and say, 'Here is how I am going to get my job done, here is how I am going to be flexible with my flexibility so on the days that you need me, I am here. Here is how I am going to get my job done and communicate. I have plenty of child care, including a backup plan.' Get it all outlined. Ask to try it out for six months and see how it goes."

By inquiring about flexible time, you are telling your employer, "I want to kick ass and give you what you need, but you need to let me give it to you in the way that I can." The reality is a majority of women never ask the question. After having a child, they don't ask for a Friday off or to work from home for a day. We cannot change policies until we at least ask for what we want. If there is enough political push from enough women who are providers for their families and demand change, it will happen. Get over your ambivalence.

Another important question to ask is whether your workplace supports women who do decide to exit the workforce and reenter after a few years. Many women who exit the workforce to have a child, or to care for a family member, find it is very challenging to reenter. Employers often have negative reactions to the gap they see in employment, especially if it is for an extended period of time. If you are in a hiring position, support women who are trying to get back into the workforce. Encourage your company to start a "returnship" program. Returnships are paid and unpaid internships that help mothers and fathers get back into the workforce after taking time off. Many organizations, including MIT, Sarah Lee, and Goldman Sachs, have created these programs, have seen success, and are now increasing the amount of returnships they offer.[50] We must recognize that an important new talent pool not only comes from India and China, but also comes from women who are reentering the workforce.

Finally, we must be aware of — and combat — the discrimination that mothers face in the workforce. Employers are less likely to hire mothers compared to women who don't have children. Oftentimes, when they make offers to women with children, their salaries are less. Not surprising, fathers don't suffer from the same penalty.[51] There is no wage gap between men with children and men without children. Again, if you are in a hiring position, be conscious of any bias you may have and encourage your peers to do the same. If you have the opportunity to hire a mother, hire her!

Invest in Women

Venture capital and political groups need to make investments in women who may not succeed the first time. Through organizations like Golden Seeds, Goldman Sachs' 10,000 Women, Astia, Kiva, Springboard Enterprises, and Accion, we can also invest in entrepreneurial women in the United States and the developing world by channeling money and resources into small businesses and their communities. You don't need to be wealthy to invest in women entrepreneurs. There are crowd-sourcing sites for women entrepreneurs like Kiva, Kickstarter, or Indiegogo, where you can donate $10 or $25 — every little bit counts.

Joanne Wilson, a prominent angel investor, has made it her business to do this, putting the majority of her investments into women-led companies. "This whole nonsensical thing of not enough women in tech, not enough women CEOs, not enough women on the board — guess what? If we invest in women entrepreneurs, we'd change the game because they're all CEOs. It's pretty easy to do," she says.

We can support women who are investing in women — women who are teaching other women the secret handshake, who are making sure they seek the right people. My friend Natalia Oberti Noguera started the Pipeline Fellowship, which trains women to be angel investors in women-led for-profit social ventures. Fellows join the program and, through mentorship and training, learn how to invest in these companies. If you want to help women entrepreneurs by investing in women-owned businesses, sign up to be a fellow or a mentor for the Pipeline Fellowship.

Also, companies like American Express OPEN, through their online websites, are helping women access organizations and resources that can help them grow their business. Count Me In's "Make Mine a Million $ Business" program encourages women to hit revenue targets of $250,000, $500,000, and $1 million.

Furthermore, as we discussed in Chapter 6, we have to encourage our sister entrepreneurs to build their networks and adopt role models who challenge them to get over their fear of failure and take risks that can increase growth. If you are an entrepreneur, mentor a rising entrepreneur. Teach her how to grow her network, introduce her to potential investors, and give her targeted advice that will teach her how to grow her business.

Encourage a Girl to Go into STEM

If we want to close the STEM gap, we've got to get girls excited about the sciences from an early age. When we launched Girls Who Code in 2012, we received support from a variety of companies and organizations, including Twitter, Google, eBay, and GE, and from influencers like Jack Dorsey and Sheryl Sandberg. This attention was humbling, but most of all, it was encouraging. It showed a need for such a program and it identified a large audience that would support it.

Classes started on July 9, 2012, and we immediately saw the potential of having more women in the technology field. On the third day, we split the girls up in teams and asked each group to come up with a product they wanted to build. All of them chose to build a mobile application. Their ideas: an app that would find family-friendly places in their neighborhood, an app to find a protest or a rally for a cause that they care about, an app to help identify the best college based on your passions and interests, an app of different tourist attractions in New York City. Each of their ideas was about helping their community; each was a way to make our lives better. Not one game — even though games are the most popular mobile app category downloaded.[52]

In just one day, the girls showed how different our world would look if we had more women with technology skills. We would have more people trying to solve everyday problems, more people focused on alleviating pain points from our lives. Which is why we have to empower girls with more education. As venture capitalist Ben Horowitz said at his talk at the Technovation Challenge 2012 Pitch Event: "If you educate a girl in the developing world, you educate five people — on average. On average, five people get educated because if you educate one girl, then she will educate at least four other people through the course of her life. That's just statistics."[53] What Ben goes on to argue is to fill the shortage we have of programmers, we are going to need more girls going into STEM, because they will train other girls!

Each of us can play a role in closing the technology gap. You can donate an old computer, iPad, or iPhone to a girl in need. You can spend time with a young girl in your life and encourage her to develop a love for science, math, technology, and engineering. The 2012 Girls Scouts study found that for girls who were interested in STEM, 65 percent of their mothers encouraged them to pursue a STEM career compared to 32 percent of girls who opted out of a STEM career.[54] Support Girls Inc., Step

Up Women's Network, or your local girls' club. Adopt a young girl as a mentee and take her to your local science museum or to a hackathon.

If you are already in this field, mentor an aspiring technologist. It is so important for girls to see someone who looks like them working in a profession they think they cannot pursue.

CONCLUSION

THE GREAT MODERN feminists — Gloria Steinem, Betty Friedan, Hillary Clinton — have brought us to a point of equality where nearly all doors are open to us. The problem now is that we are not walking through them fast enough. Gloria, Betty, and leaders of the modern feminist movement fought tirelessly for the rights and empowerment that many of us enjoy. Feminists of the 1960s and 1970s overtly and radically challenged many patriarchal and sexist institutions and policies that today's women no longer have to face.

We cannot forget that past. In order to know where were headed, we first have to know where we've been. The problems that earlier generations of feminists set out to fix (control over our bodies, equal pay, gender parity, etc.) still exist. Now, it is time for modern-day women's rights advocates to put forth new models to confront these challenges. We have to spread the message to women across the nation — stop waiting to rule the world. There is no single-file line.

The most important lesson I've learned, and that I hope I've imparted to you, is that before we can change the inequities women face, we must change ourselves. We must really look at ourselves and explore what holds us back individually and examine how we may consciously or unconsciously be holding one another back.

This begins with you. Work through your aversion to risk and failure. Don't quell your ambition, but embrace it — and scream it from the mountaintops. As members of the sisterhood, we must put aside our judgment of one another and genuinely support and uplift each other

In the years since my first election, I have taken these lessons to heart and learned so much about myself and the type of leader I want to be, the type of leadership I want to inspire.

And in the process, I have learned how to be me. How to speak like me, dress like me, and connect like me. I am no longer concerned with making a perfect speech. I no longer find myself frantically reading through the comment section of new stories written about me, worrying about what others think and say.

I openly share my doubts, my vulnerabilities, and my emotions. I express my pain and ask for help to achieve my dreams. By being open, and inclusive, and real, I have found a vibrant community of women just like me; I have gained a sisterhood of women who have my back, and I have theirs. I have enriched my career and life and I have seen the world that I want my unborn daughter to live in.

I have worked with and been inspired by others, every day, to help create the world I want the next generation to live in. As women we must have the humility to see the world as it is, but the audacity to envision it as it could be. To apply a new lens of female leadership and reinvent, reshape, and retool the traditional system. To realize that we can learn from the poorest of women and the richest of women. We can and should be talking to one another about what this new model should look like — and about how we can build it together.

Today's women's movement is progressing in a completely

different way than it has in the past. Our leaders are not ashamed to leverage and champion one another. And guys? We aren't hating on them; we are looking to men to be our allies.

We no longer see them as a barrier to our success.

I wrote this book as a challenge to the next generation of women to think about leadership differently. I asked you to celebrate competition, pursue failure, build your sisterhood, and to free yourself from believing that you have to behave like anyone other than yourself. I encouraged you to find strength in your gender instead of trying to hide or apologize for it. I reminded you that you can be anything, and that being a woman has very little to do with the ability to achieve. As Hilary Mason, my friend and the chief scientist of bit.ly, said, "I want to be the best coder, not the best female coder."

Most of all, I wrote this book because I wanted to tell you to pursue your dreams. There are opportunities for all of us — not just for one of us at a time — and you must pursue them with all of your energy. And acknowledge the fact that you are not alone — allow others to assist in the pursuit of your dreams and help others achieve theirs. The sisterhood is a powerful thing, and in the twenty-first century, sponsorship is the new feminism.

This is how we will spark systemic change that will move women and girls ahead, and ultimately change the world. Together we can create the world we want to live it.

We all have an inner activist. Awaken this spirit in yourself and inspire other women to do the same — enlist them in remaking America. Change the way you think about leadership, how you apply for jobs, how you teach your daughters, how big you dream, and the steps you take to get there. You don't have to wait. Your time is now.

ACKNOWLEDGMENTS

THE FIRST HONORABLE MENtion is to my husband, Nihal Mehta, for being the best partner a woman could ask for. His constant love, support, and encouragement enables me to pursue my dreams to the fullest extent. Thank you, Nihal, for bothering me when I needed to take a break and for giving me the room to write when I really needed to write.

I couldn't have written this book if not for my constant companion, Stanley the Puppy. For over a year, Stan without hesitation woke up with me in early hours to write and provided me with countless encouragement. She nudged me with her nose, to move forward during the hard parts.

I want to thank my parents, Mukund and Meena, for teaching me to be resilient and to reach for the stars. I know coming to this country and building a life for us was never easy, and I thank you for the sacrifices you made for me and Keshma. To my sister, Keshma, thank you for being the first sister in my sisterhood.

I could not have written this book if women didn't open up their hearts and heads during this journey to help me uncover the new model for female leadership. I would like to thank all the women who shared their experiences with me: Tiffany Dufu, Stephanie Harbour, Joanne Wilson, Nomiki Konst, Susan Lyne, Libby Brittain, Vivene Labaton, Richelle Parham, Raphaela Sapire, Susan McPherson, Katie Stanton, Beth Comstock, Julie Ruvolo, Anne-Marie Slaughter, Betsy Morgan, Rachel Sklar, Kathryn Minshew, Blair Miller, Mary Ellen Iskenderian, Ty Stiklorius, Randi Zuckerberg, Whitney Johnson, Clara Shih, Marie Wilson, Sara Haider, Audrey MacClean, Anu Duggal, Archana Chatta, Jenna Arnold, Lisa Witter, Diana Taylor, Chloe Drew, Shaherose Charania, Niamh Hughes and the Sandbox crew, Sarah Robb O-Hagan, Cali Yost, Ashley Bush, Natalia Oberti Noguera, and Mika Brzezinski.

I want to especially thank the women who helped me put my vision to paper. Vinca LaFleur and Sarada Peri from West Wing Writers, two in a million writers who every author should hire if they want an innovative team that will help them bring their story to life. Their brilliant feedback and encouragement helped me write a book that will not only help young women rise up and lead, but one that I can be proud of for decades to come. They put more time in helping me write this book than was asked of them, and I will forever be grateful for their contribution to the sisterhood. I also want to thank the incredible Caryle Adler. She joined me in the beginning and at the end of my journey in writing this book. As a first-time author, I didn't know where to start or how to end, and I couldn't have done it without her guidance and brilliant writing and editing skills. Another honorable MENtion to Ben Yarrow (who helped me find Vinca, Sarada, and Caryle) and a special thanks to Allison Yarrow and Deepa Varadarajan, who reviewed and edited chapters, providing me critical input and feedback.

I want to thank Amazon's team for being the ultimate sisterhood. There is no way I would have ever written this book without Julia Cheiffetz suggesting it and pushing me every step of the way. Katie Salisbury was the ultimate partner in crime as an editor, and I would never have finished this book without her. Also thanks to Larry Kirshbaum, Courtney Dodson, Maggie Sivon, Alexandra Woodworth, Alicia Criner, and Anna Riego.

Thank you to Rebecca Rattner, who spent a great deal of her time helping me remember every last story and compiling research and ideas. Rebecca is a great example of the next generation of young female leaders who I know will make an incredible impact in this country. Thank you to my research assistants Sarah Belfer, Shelby Maniccia, and Neha Uberoi, and a special thank you to the fabulous Gloria Noel, who is a phenomenal researcher and simply a superstar.

This book would not be possible without those who have believed in and supported me, including my supporters from my 2010 campaign, my interns, and my staff, including James Allen, Kunal Modi, Kane Sarhan, Nancy Bright, Dabash Negash, and Charlotte Stone.

I want to also thank Congressman Carolyn Maloney. Congresswoman Maloney has been a tireless supporter of women's rights and she is one of the women whose shoulders we all stand on. Thank you for your graciousness after my election and for giving me the opportunity to find my passion.

I extend my greatest respect and thanks to my mentors, including the late Leon Higginbotham Jr. and Hillary Clinton, who have all inspired me to commit my life to public service. I aspire to be half as great of a leader as Hillary Clinton is, and without the example you have set for me and countless other women, I would not be where I am today.

I want to also thank a special group of women who have had

a major impact on my life and showed me the importance of vertical and horizontal mentors and sponsors. First, Maureen White, who was the finance chair of the Democratic National Committee for many years. Since 2002, when I first met her, I literally watched and learned from her and how she used her passion for building the party to bring about real change. She, like Hillary, constantly mentored and helped women. I learned about the importance of women's empowerment in immigrant communities from women like Romita Shetty, who was a part of a small group of South Asian women who started SAKHI, an organization to help South Asian victims of domestic violence. She became a big sister, always supporting me and opening her home and networks to me, giving me advice, lending a hand. Another important mentor has been Cathy Lasry, who took a huge leap in supporting my campaign. She would always stand up and support me, take the hits, and constantly champion me. I would not be able to even opine on this topic if not for Marie Wilson. When I told Marie Wilson, the founder of the White House Project, that I was thinking of running she looked at me and smiled and said, "Reshma, the best reason for running is if you think you can do a better job, so run." Instead of dissuading me from running for office, she helped me believe in myself. In supporting me, when so many of her peers did not, Marie exercised an incredible amount of courage and loyalty that I will never forget. Marie embodies the power of the sisterhood because she showed how having even just one woman there to hold your hand and tell you that you can do something impossible can help you do just that.

Thank you to the women who are part of my peer network, my hook-up sisters who I rely on daily for support and advice: Tiffany Dufu, Chloe Drew, Trina DasGupta, Annie Mullaly, Madhu Goel, June Sarpong, Dee Poku, Sumana Setty, and Anu

Duggal. These women are there for me to help me build my business plan for Girls Who Code or the strategic plan for my next campaign. We support each other and offer our networks and resources to help one another pursue our dreams. I want to also thank my political sister, Krystal Ball, a former congressional candidate and currently an anchor on MSNBC. When we were running for Congress in 2010, we leaned on each other during our races, and provided support and encouragement when we couldn't find it elsewhere. I want to also thank my executive director for Girls Who Code, Kristen Titus. I look forward to building the movement with you!

Finally I want to thank my two nieces, Maya and Surina Hogan, for being the inspiration for this book. I hold your two adorable faces in my mind and heart as I fight to make this world a place where you will never have to wait in line.

NOTES

INTRODUCTION

1 Mitchell, Lesa. "Overcoming the Gender Gap: Women Entrepreneurs as Economic Drivers." Ewing Marion Kauffman Foundation. September 2011.

1. FAIL FAST, FAIL FIRST, FAIL HARD

1 Miller, Claire Cain. "For Incoming I.B.M. Chief, Self-Confidence Is Rewarded." *New York Times.* October 27, 2011.
2 "IBM's Ginni Rometty: Growth and Comfort Do Not Coexist." *Fortune's* Most Powerful Women Summit. *Fortune.* October 5, 2011.
3 Zweig, Jason. "For Mother's Day, Give Her Reins to the Portfolio." *Wall Street Journal.* May 9, 2009.
4 Lewis, Anna. "When Programming Was Considered Women's Work." *Cap Times.* September 5, 2011.
5 Ibid.
6 "Men and Equality, Women and Leadership." Episode 2. *Broad Experience.* April 15, 2012. Available at http://www.thebroadexperience.com/listen/2012/4/26/episode-two-men-and-equality-women-and-leadership.html.
7 Latman, Richard Keith. *The Good Fail: Entrepreneurial Lessons from the Rise and Fall of Microworkz.* Hoboken, NJ: John Wiley and Sons, 2012.
8 Wilson, Joanne. "Making It: My Address to the 2012 Women Entrepreneurs Festival." Huffington Post. January 19, 2012.
9 Murphy, Patricia. "The Next 10 Women to Watch in Politics." *Politics Daily.* July 8, 2010.
10 Pressfield, Steven. *The War of Art: Break Through the Blocks and Win Your Inner Creative Battles.* New York: Warner Books, 2002.
11 Buck, Stephanie. "How Gen Y Women Fare in Today's Workplace." Mashable. March 7, 2012.
12 Streib, Lauren. "Producer Nina Jacobson Gambles on 'Hunger Games.'" Daily Beast. March 12, 2012.

13 "Generation X: Overlooked and Hugely Important, Finds New Study from
     the Center for Work-Life Policy." Press release. Center for Work-Life Policy.
     September 16, 2011.

2. UNAPOLOGETICALLY AMBITIOUS

1   Medina, Jennifer. "In House Race, Maloney Defeats Primary Rival." *New
     York Times.* September 15, 2010.
2   Groer, Annie. "N.Y. Rep. Carolyn Maloney vs. Reshma Saujani: Incumbent
     vs. Upstart." *Politics Daily.* June 13, 2010.
3   Barrett, Wayne. "Reshma Saujani's Road to Congress? Right Down Wall
     Street. Let Me Be Your Guide." *Village Voice.* August 23, 2010.
4   "Law Firm Diversity Wobbles: Minority Numbers Bounce Back While
     Women Associates Extend Two-Year Decline." Press release. Association for
     Legal Career Professionals. November 3, 2011.
5   *Report of the Sixth Annual National Survey on Retention and Promotion of
     Women in Law Firms.* National Association of Women Lawyers and the
     NAWL Foundation. October 2011.
6   "Women in Medicine." Catalyst. April 23, 2012. Available at http://www.
     catalyst.org/knowledge/women-medicine.
7   Freischlag, Julie A. "Women Surgeons — Still in a Male-Dominated World."
     Yale Journal of Biology and Medicine 81, no. 4 (December 2008): 203–4.
8   Soares, Rachel, et al. *2011 Catalyst Census: Fortune 500 Women Executive
     Officers and Top Earners.* Catalyst. December 13, 2011. Available at http://
     www.catalyst.org/knowledge/2011-catalyst-census-fortune-500-women-
     executive-officers-and-top-earners.
9   "Percent of Faculty in Tenure-Track Appointments and Percent of Faculty
     with Tenure, by Affiliation, Academic Rank, and Gender, 2011–12." American
     Association of University Professors. 2012.
10 Belkin, Lisa. "The Opt-Out Revolution." *New York Times.* October 26,
     2003.
11 Barsh, Joanna, and Lareina Yee. *Unlocking the Full Potential of Women in the
     U.S. Economy. Wall Street Journal* Executive Task Force for Women in the
     Economy. McKinsey and Company. 2011.
12 Saad, Lydia. "Stay at Home Moms in US Lean Independent, Lower Income."
     April 19, 2012. Available at http://www.gallup.com/poll/153995/stay-home-
     moms-lean-independent-lower-income.aspx.
13 Locks, Jesse, and Elisa Parker. "See Jane Do: Tiffany Dufu." *Union.* April 22,
     2011.

14 Anderson, Melissa J. "Women, Age, and Ambition — A Fresh Perspective." Glass Hammer. November 22, 2011.

15 Meyer, Harvey. "Fathers Know Best." Human Resource Executive Online. October 16, 2011.

16 "Exclusive Interview with Facebook Leadership: Mark Zuckerberg, CEO/ Co-Founder & Sheryl Sandberg, COO." *Charlie Rose*. PBS. November 7, 2011.

17 Seymour, Lesley Jane. "Women's Ambition: A Surprising Report." *More*. November 9, 2011. Available at http://www.more.com/flexible-job-survey.

18 Caprino, Kathy. "Busting the Myth that Women Are Less Ambitious than Men." *Forbes*. November 28, 2011.

19 Wolfe, Ira S. "Trophy Kids: What Goes Around Comes Around!" *HR: The Human Resource*. February–March 2011.

20 Asthana, Anushka. "They Don't Live for Work . . . They Work to Live." *London Guardian*. May 24, 2008.

21 Barrett, Kara Nichols. *Gen Y Women in the Workplace*. Business and Professional Women's Foundation. April 2011.

22 Fels, Anna. *Necessary Dreams: Ambition in Women's Changing Lives*. New York: Pantheon Books, 2004.

23 Dowd, Maureen. "Obama's Big Screen Test." *New York Times*. February 21, 2007.

24 Applebaum, Anne. "Irrational Ambition Is Hillary Clinton's Flaw." *London Telegraph*. May 8, 2008.

25 Copeland, Libby. "How to Hit a Woman." *Slate*. November 22, 2011.

26 Collins, Gerald. "Hillary Clinton Is Too Ambitious to Be the First Female President." *Onion*. May 24, 2006.

27 "Stepping Stone." *New York Post*. November 20, 2011.

28 Monhollon, Tiffany. "Ambition and the Tale of One Generation Y Woman." Blog entry. Little Red Suit. June 29, 2007. Available at http://littleredsuit. com/2007/06/29/ambition-and-the-tale-of-one-generation-y-woman/.

29 Barsh, Joanna, Susie Cranston, and Geoffrey Lewis. *How Remarkable Women Lead: The Breakthrough Model for Work and Life*. New York: Crown Business, 2009.

3. DON'T WORRY IF THEY DON'T LIKE YOU

1 Free to Be You and Me Foundation. http://www.freetobefoundation.org/ index.htm.

2 Barbie Liberation Organization. http://sniggle.net/barbie.php.

3 Beck, Koa. "Disney's New Princess Is a Little Girl, Will Teach 'Lessons.'" Mommyish.com. December 13, 2011.

4 "'Princess Play' Presents Opportunity to Teach Girls Good Manners." *Inside Vandy.* August 16, 2011.

5 White, Kate. *Why Good Girls Don't Get Ahead . . . but Gutsy Girls Do: Nine Secrets Every Career Woman Must Know.* New York: Warner Books, 1995.

6 Rojahn, Krystyna, and Tineke M. Willemsen. "The Evaluation of Effectiveness and Likability of Gender-Role Congruent and Gender-Role Incongruent Leaders." *Sex Roles* 30, nos. 1–2 (January 1994): 109–19.

7 *The Double-Bind Dilemma for Women in Leadership: Damned if You Do, Doomed if You Don't.* Catalyst. July 15, 2007. Available at http://www.catalyst.org/knowledge/double-bind-dilemma-women-leadership-damned-if-you-do-doomed-if-you-dont-0.

8 Simmons, Jacqueline, and Elisa Martinuzzi. "Davos Women Minority of One as Sandberg Shares with Bossy Girls." Bloomberg. January 30, 2012.

9 Ball, Sarah, Jessica Bennett, and Jesse Ellison. "Are We There Yet?" Daily Beast. March 18, 2010.

10 Ibid.

11 Babcock, Linda, and Sara Laschever. *Women Don't Ask: Negotiation and the Gender Divide.* Princeton, NJ: Princeton University Press, 2003.

12 Ibid.

13 Crenshaw, Dorothy. "If PR Is a Woman's World, Why Do We Earn Less?" Crenshaw Communications. March 8, 2011.

14 Schneider, Andrea Kupfer, Catherine H. Tinsley, Sandra Cheldelin, and Emily T. Amanatullah. "Likeability v. Competence: The Impossible Choice Faced by Female Politicians, Attenuated by Lawyers." *Duke Journal of Gender Law and Policy* 17 (2010): 363–84.

15 Ball, Bennett, and Ellison. "Are We There Yet?"

16 Brush, Candida, et al. *Gatekeepers of Venture Growth: A Diana Project Report on the Role and Participation of Women in the Venture Capital Industry.* Ewing Marion Kauffman Foundation. 2004. Available at http://www.kauffman.org/research-and-policy/gatekeepers-of-venture-growth.aspx.

17 Carter, Nancy M., and Christine Silva. *The Myth of the Ideal Worker: Does Doing All the Right Things Really Get Women Ahead?* Catalyst. October 1, 2011. Available at http://www.catalyst.org/knowledge/myth-ideal-worker-does-doing-all-right-things-really-get-women-ahead.

18 Johnson, Whitney. "Can 'Nice Girls' Negotiate?" HBR Blog Network.

Harvard Business Review. December 2, 2009. Available at http://blogs.hbr.
org/cs/2009/12/can_nice_girls_negotiate.html.

4. FOLLOW YOUR BLISS

1 Civian, Jan. "Critical Talent and the New Career Paradigm: Some Industry
   Insights." American Business Collaboration for Quality Dependent Care.
   April 2007.

2 Rampell, Catherine. "Women May Earn Less, but They Find Their Work
   More Meaningful." *New York Times.* February 16, 2012.

3 Godin, Seth. *The Dip: A Little Book that Teaches You When to Quit (and
   When to Stick).* New York: Portfolio, 2007.

4 McKay, Dawn Rosenberg. "Job Burnout." About.com. Accessed March 17,
   2013. Available at http://careerplanning.about.com/od/workrelated/a/
   burnout.htm.

5 Helgesen, Sally, and Julie Johnson. *The Female Vision: Women's Real Power at
   Work.* San Francisco, CA: Berrett-Koehler Publishers, 2010.

5. BE AUTHENTIC

1 Rubinstein, Dana. "Fresh-Faced Reshma and the Assault on Fortress
   Maloney." *New York Observer.* May 5, 2010.

2 Dominus, Susan. "Blazing Campaign Trails in a Certain 3-Inch Heel." *New
   York Times.* August 23, 2010.

3 Harragan, Betty. *Games Mother Never Taught You: Corporate Gamesmanship
   for Women.* New York: Rawson Associates, 1977.

4 Valenti, Jessica. "Material Culture, Feminist Activism, and the Future of Feminism." Blog entry. Historiann. June 6, 2011. Available at http://www.histori
   ann.com/2011/06/06/material-culture-feminist-activism-and-the-future-of-
   feminism/.

5 Gilmer, Ellen M. "They Gave Women Pantsuits, but Equal Footing Is Yet
   to Come." Redorbit. March 9, 2012. Available at http://www.redorbit.com/
   news/space/1112490373/they-gave-women-pantsuits-but-equal-footing-is-
   yet-to-come/.

6 Breanne, Nicole. "Can Feminists Like Fashion?" Blog entry. Zelda Lily. February 5, 2012. Available at http://zeldalily.com/index.php/2012/02/can-fem
   inists-like-fashion/.

7 Kolakowski, Mark. "How to Dress for Interviews." About.com. Accessed

March 17, 2013. Available at http://financecareers.about.com/od/
interviewing/a/Dress_For_Interviews.htm.

8 Miller, Claire Cain. "Techies Break a Fashion Taboo." *New York Times.*
August 3, 2012.

9 "Up in Arms: Michelle Obama's Sleeveless Style Sparks Controversy."
Huffington Post. March 30, 2009.

10 Chang, Bee-Shyuan. "Outfitting the 'Veep.'" *New York Times.* April 25, 2012.

11 Parker, Suzi. "Hillary Clinton, Barefaced and in Politics." *Washington Post.*
May 8, 2012.

12 Ibid.

13 McDevitt, Caitlin. "Hillary Clinton on Make-up, Hair: Who Cares?"
Politico. May 8, 2012.

14 Giridharadas, Anand. "New Leaders Find Strength in Diversity." *New York
Times.* May 6, 2010.

15 Chee, Angela. "Indra Nooyi: Powerful Woman, Powerful Mother, and Her
Secrets to Success." Blog entry. Zen Mom. August 12, 2011. Available at
http://thezenmom.com/2011/08/12/indra-nooyi-powerful-woman
-powerful-mother-and-her-secrets-to-success/.

16 Frankel, Barbara. "PepsiCo's Indra Nooyi: 'I Am a Walking Example of
Diversity.'" *DiversityInc.* May 2008.

17 "'Macho' Women Face Backlash at Work, Researchers Find." Science*Daily.*
January 19, 2011.

18 Brzezinski, Mika. *Knowing Your Value: Women, Money, and Getting What
You're Worth.* New York: Weinstein Books, 2010.

19 Ibid.

20 Ibid.

21 Zenger, Jack, and Joseph Folkman. "Gender Shouldn't Matter, but
Apparently It Still Does." HBR Blog Network. *Harvard Business Review.*
April 4, 2012. Available at http://blogs.hbr.org/cs/2012/04/gender_
shouldnt_matter_but_app.html.

22 Zenger, Jack, and Joseph Folkman. "Are Women Better Leaders than Men?"
HBR Blog Network. *Harvard Business Review.* March 15, 2012. Available at
http://blogs.hbr.org/cs/2012/03/a_study_in_leadership_women_do.html.

23 Patten, Eileen, and Kim Parker. "A Gender Reversal on Career Aspirations."
Pew Research Center: Social and Demographic Trends. April 19, 2012.

24 Bronson, Po, and Ashley Merryman. "Housework." Factbook. Accessed
March 17, 2013. Available at http://www.pobronson.com/factbook/
pages/278.html.

25 Steinem, Gloria. *Revolution from Within: A Book of Self-Esteem*. Boston: Little, Brown, 1992.

26 Patten and Parker. "A Gender Reversal on Career Aspirations."

27 Kohan, Eddie Gehman. "President Obama on Fatherhood: Yes to Family Dinners, and No to Boys with Beer." Blog entry. Obama Foodorama. June 17, 2011. Available at http://obamafoodorama.blogspot.com/2011/06/president-obama-on-fatherhood-yes-to.html.

28 Patten and Parker. "A Gender Reversal on Career Aspirations."

29 Martinez, Gladys, Kimberly Daniels, and Anjani Chandra. "Fertility of Men and Women Aged 15–44 Years in the United States: National Survey of Family Growth." *National Health Statistics Report* 51 (April 12, 2012): 1–28.

30 Sarton, May. *Journal of a Solitude*. New York: W. W. Norton, 1972.

6. BUILDING A SISTERHOOD FOR THE TWENTY-FIRST CENTURY

1 "More Working Women than Men Have College Degrees, Census Bureau Reports." Press release. United States Census Bureau. April 26, 2011.

2 Luscombe, Belinda. "Woman Power: The Rise of the Sheconomy." *Time*. November 22, 2010.

3 La Ferla, Ruth. "How to Move Up? The Sorority Track." *New York Times*. July 13, 2003.

4 Anderson, Melissa J. "How Sponsorship Can Help Senior Women Break the Marzipan Ceiling." Glass Hammer. January 19, 2011.

5 Holland, Stephanie. "Marketing to Women Quick Facts." Blog entry. Sheconomy. Accessed March 17, 2013. Available at http://www.she-conomy.com/facts-on-women.

6 Luscombe. "Woman Power: The Rise of the Sheconomy."

7 "Title IX, Education Amendments of 1972." U.S. Department of Labor.

8 "The Equal Pay Act of 1963." U.S. Equal Opportunity Commission.

9 Rezvani, Selena. "Not Your Mother's Ambition." *Washington Post*. May 13, 2011.

10 Jones, Del. "Often, Men Help Women Get to the Corner Office." *USA Today*. August 5, 2009.

11 Hewlett, Sylvia Ann. "The Real Benefit of Finding a Sponsor." HBR Blog Network. *Harvard Business Review*. January 26, 2011. Available at http://blogs.hbr.org/hbr/hewlett/2011/01/the_real_benefit_of_finding_a.html.

12 Naziri, Jessica. "Women Start-ups Lack Access to Venture Capital." CNBC. October 10, 2011.

13 Stampler, Laura. "Office Sponsors Needed, but Lacking for Women in the
    Workplace: Study." Huffington Post. August 17, 2011.

14 Interview with Herminia Ibarra. "Women Are Over-Mentored (but Under-
    Sponsored)." HBR IdeaCast. *Harvard Business Review.* August 26, 2010.

15 Lang, Ilene H. "The Ambition Gap Myth." Blog entry. Catalyst. January
    5, 2012. Available at http://catalyst.cmm-zoo.com/blog/catalyzing/
    ambition-gap-myth.

16 Vance, Ashlee. "At Xerox, a Transition for the Record Books." *New York
    Times.* May 21, 2009.

17 Sanbonmatsu, Kira, Susan J. Carroll, and Debbie Walsh. *Poised to Run:
    Women's Pathways to the State Legislatures.* Center for American Women and
    Politics. Eagleton Institute of Politics, Rutgers University, New Jersey. 2009.

18 Beth Reingold, *The Uneven Presence of Women and Minorities in America's
    State Legislatures and Why It Matters.* Scholars Strategy Network. 2012.

19 ChicConnect. www.chicconnect.org.

20 "Year of the Republican Woman? Yes and No." Press release. CAWP Election
    Watch. Center for American Women and Politics. Eagleton Institute of
    Politics, Rutgers University, New Jersey. September 20, 2010.

21 Thomas, Louisa. "Are You Ambitious Enough?" *Marie Claire.* September 27,
    2010.

7. TAKING IT TO THE STREETS

1 Sandgren, Melissa. "For Struggling Boards, the Answer May Be Closer
   than You Think," in "Unleashing Change: Stimulus, Sit-Ins, and Systemic
   Reform." *Kennedy School Review.* 2012.

2 Hegewisch, Ariane, Claudia Williams, and Angela Edwards. *The Gender
   Wage Gap: 2012.* Institute for Women's Policy Research. Updated March
   2013. Available at http://www.iwpr.org/initiatives/pay-equity-and-
   discrimination.

3 *The Simple Truth about the Gender Pay Gap.* American Association of
   University Women. 2013.

4 Hegewisch, Williams, and Edwards. *The Gender Wage Gap.*

5 *The Simple Truth about the Gender Pay Gap.*

6 Hegewisch, Williams, and Edwards. *The Gender Wage Gap.*

7 Moughari, Layla, Rhiana Gunn-Wright, and Barbara Gault. *Gender
   Segregation in Fields of Study at Community Colleges and Implications for
   Future Earnings.* Institute for Women's Policy Research. April 2012.

8 Ibid.

9   *The State of Women-Owned Businesses Report.* American Express OPEN.
    Accessed March 17, 2013. Available at https://c401345.ssl.cf1.rackcdn.com/
    pdf/State_of_Women-Owned_Businesses-Report_FINAL.pdf.

10 *Women-Owned Businesses in the 21st Century.* White House Council on
    Women and Girls. Economics and Statistics Administration, U.S. Depart-
    ment of Commerce. October 2010.

11 *The State of Women-Owned Businesses Report.*

12 "Women-Owned Business Facts." Womens Business Center. Accessed March
    17, 2013. Available at http://www.wbc-rgv.org/?page_id=268.

13 Yost, Cali Williams. "3 Reasons Why Card-Carrying Capitalists Should
    Support Paid Family Leave." *Forbes.* May 23, 2012.

14 Ibid.

15 Ayanna, Ariel Meysam. "Aggressive Parental Leave Incentivizing: A Statutory
    Proposal Toward Gender Equalization in the Workplace." *University of Penn-
    sylvania Journal of Labor and Employment Law* 9, no. 2 (2007): 293–324.

16 Fass, Sarah. *Paid Leave in the States: A Critical Support for Low-Wage Workers
    and Their Families.* National Center for Children in Poverty. March 2009.

17 Galinsky, Ellen, Kerstin Aumann, and James T. Bond. *Times Are Changing:
    Gender and Generation at Work and at Home.* Families and Work Institute.
    August 2011.

18 *Women in America: Indicators of Social and Economic Well-Being.* White
    House Council on Women and Girls. Economics and Statistics Administra-
    tion, U.S. Department of Commerce. Office of Management and Budget, Ex-
    ecutive Office of the President. March 2011.

19 Shoemaker, Jolynn, Amy Brown, and Rachel Barbour. "A Revolutionary
    Change: Making the Workplace More Flexible." *Solutions* 2, no. 2 (February
    2011).

20 "Additional Child Care Funding Is Essential to Stop State Cuts." National
    Women's Law Center. July 12, 2012.

21 Wohlsen, Marcus. "Women Engineers Trace Tech Gender Gap to Child-
    hood" Huffington Post. June 4, 2012.

22 Women, Minorities, and Persons with Disabilities in Science and
    Engineering. National Science Foundation. February 2013. Available at
    http://www.nsf.gov/statistics/wmpd/2013/digest/theme2_3.cfm.

23 Beede, David, et al. "Women in STEM: A Gender Gap to Innovation." Issue
    brief #04-11. Economics and Statistics Administration, U.S. Department of
    Commerce. August 2011.

24 Anderson, Melissa J. "Why STEM Needs Women." Glass Hammer. August
    5, 2011.

25 Beede et al. "Women in STEM: A Gender Gap to Innovation."

26 Cohoon, Joanne McGrath. "Wanted: Technical Women." *U.S. News and World Report.* January 3, 2012.

27 Langdon, David, et al. "STEM: Good Jobs Now and for the Future." Issue brief #03-11. Economics and Statistics Administration, U.S. Department of Commerce. July 2011.

28 Ibid.

29 Corbett, Christianne. "The Pay Gap in STEM Fields." Forum topic. Scitable. April 2012. Available at http://www.nature.com/scitable/forums/women-in-science/the-pay-gap-in-stem-fields-19116412.

30 Fleischman, Howard L., et al. *Highlights from PISA 2009: Performance of U.S. 15-Year-Old Students in Reading, Mathematics, and Science Literacy in an International Context.* National Center for Education Statistics, Institute of Education Sciences, U.S. Department of Education. December 2010.

31 Shettle, Carolyn, et al. *America's High School Graduates: Results from the 2005 NAEP High School Transcript Study.* National Center for Education Statistics, Institute of Education Sciences, U.S. Department of Education. February 2007.

32 Modi, Kamla, Judy Schoenberg, and Kimberlee Salmond. *Generation STEM: What Girls Say about Science, Technology, Engineering, and Math.* Girl Scout Research Institute. 2012.

33 "ACM-WGBH Finds Large Gender Gap in Teens Interested in Computing as a Career." Press release. Association for Computing Machinery. June 2, 2009.

34 Modi, Schoenberg, and Salmond. *Generation STEM.*

35 Ibid.

36 Hafner, Katie. "Giving Women the Access Code." *New York Times.* April 2, 1012.

37 Modi, Schoenberg, and Salmond. *Generation STEM.*

38 Crawford, Susan P. "The New Digital Divide." *New York Times.* December 3, 2011.

39 "The Campaign Against Women." Editorial. *New York Times.* May 19, 2012.

40 "Choice-Related Laws in the States." NARAL Pro-Choice America. Accessed March 17, 2013. Available at http://www.prochoiceamerica.org/what-is-choice/fast-facts/.

41 "The Campaign Against Women." *New York Times.*

42 "State Policy Trends: Abortion and Contraception in the Crosshairs." Guttmacher Institute. April 13, 2012.

43 "The Campaign Against Women." *New York Times.*

44 Bassett, Laura. "Tom Corbett, Pennsylvania Governor, on Ultrasound Mandate: Just 'Close Your Eyes.'" Huffington Post. March 15, 2012.

45 Salganicoff, Alina, and Usha Ranji. "Insurance Coverage of Contraceptives." Henry J. Kaiser Family Foundation. February 21, 2012. Available at http://policyinsights.kff.org/2012/february/insurance-coverage-of-contraceptives.aspx.

46 Kelley, Angela Maria, and Philip E Wolgin. "10 Facts You Need to Know About Immigrant Women." Center for American Progress. March 7, 2012.

47 Ibid.

48 Batalova, Jeanne. "Immigrant Women in the United States." Migration Policy Institute. December 2009.

49 "The DREAM Act." Immigration Policy Center. Updated May 18, 2011. Available at http://www.immigrationpolicy.org/just-facts/dream-act.

50 Ryan, Jill. "'Returnships' Offer Path to Jobs for Stay-at-Home Moms." *Here and Now.* July 20, 2011.

51 *The Simple Truth about the Gender Pay Gap.*

52 Whitney, Lance. "Games Reign as Most Popular Mobile Apps." CNET. July 6, 2011.

53 Horowitz, Ben. "The Future of Humankind Is Dependent on Technovation Girls." Lecture. Technovation Challenge 2012 Pitch Event. Mountain View, California. April 28, 2012. Available at http://www.youtube.com/watch?v=wQnDDKDiSy8.

54 Modi, Schoenberg, and Salmond. *Generation STEM.*